Learning to Understand Cultures

An Introduction
to Intercultural Encounters

Heike Tiedeck

ISBN 978-3-95776-199-6

Picture credited to David Pisnoy

Cover designed by Rebekka Choo

Translation from German (Kulturen verstehen lernen, ISBN 978-3-95776-127-9) by Joseph M. Barnes

Contents

Foreword

It is said by many that in our generation the world has become a 'global village'. With the news media, the internet and social media platforms it now means that nowhere or no-one is far away. This is why the question is asked all across our world on a daily basis – "Why don't they do it properly?"

The answer to that question finds its response in this book. In a 'village' everybody does everything the same way but the same is not true of our 'global village'. The reason is – 'Culture'!

This book challenges the concept that to 'do it properly' means to 'do it the way *I* do it'.

The large majority of people believe that the way they conduct themselves is the best way. And they are right – for themselves. However, as John Dunne wrote – "No man is an island" and merely to live means that we have to interact with others. But that is the point at which problems arise because our differences are mainly due to the culture in which we were raised.

'Global villagers' are people who are aware of the behavioural why and how of others whilst they themselves respond by being flexible and willing to adapt. This in turn will bring peace and harmony into otherwise discordant situations.

As missionaries for eight years in Ghana, West Africa, my wife and I spent the first year observing, listening and asking questions in order to help us understand our 'differences'. Maybe this was why we were eventually described as "Ghanaians in white skin".

Heike Tiedeck is not only a theorist but, more importantly, a practitioner. She brings to this book so many personal practical examples that support the theory, which makes it all the more readable and all the more useful to help us personally apply what she has written.

The Biblical Perspectives are a helpful addition because they give a holistic viewpoint from "the God and Father of us all".

Unless we are challenged on these matters – which this book does and does well – we will continue to upset others and allow ourselves to be disturbed within our communities.

This is not a casual read. It is a book to be read, studied and applied in order to overcome the multitude of differences that we all encounter, as daily we walk through our 'global village'.

I highly recommend this cultural wake-up call. May God help us to be 'doers of these words and not just readers'.

Reverend Robert Lionel Currie
November 2020

Preface

As a youngster I had pen-pals all around the globe. When I turned eighteen, I travelled to Ireland to visit one of them; at age nineteen, I spent ten months in France as an au-pair in a French family. A year later I began to study social sciences with the aim to become an ambassador. I wanted to live abroad.

From an early age I was fascinated by foreign cultures and languages, and I am thankful that through the years I have been able to meet people from many different cultures; some of whom have become good friends. They made me see how German I am; that being German involves strengths and weaknesses, and that learning from those who are different makes for an enriching life experience.

Many of my intercultural encounters and experiences only made sense, though, when I began to deal with the topic of culture in a theoretical way. With that theoretical framework in place I enjoy observing and discovering cultural differences even more.

Yet, things foreign to us can sometimes be a little unsettling. As a small child I once met an African man when my family was shopping in the city. Afraid I held onto my mum's skirt and hid behind it. When my family lived in Ghana thirty years later, I observed the same behaviour in the local children who had never seen a white person. Our five-year old son – who at that time had spent most of his life in Africa – was completely confused when at the airport in Accra he saw the dressed-up British stewardesses in black tights: "Mum, why are they white on the top and black on the bottom?"

There are many things that people of all cultures have in common, but there is also a lot that is so different that it can lead to grave misunderstandings. Teachers encourage **"multiple intelligences"**[1] in their students. In a globalized world *intercultural* **intelligence**[2] needs to be part of it.

With this book I want to assist in understanding cultures. I want to encourage intercultural encounters.

I developed the book from teaching material I use for lectures. That is why you will find little learning exercises that you can use on your own or with others as small tasks for self-discovery. I tried to use many illustrations to make the theory come alive. As I am a Christian and many of my readers will

---

[1] Developed in the 1980s by Howard Gardner the theory of multiple intelligences is still a pedagogical concept today. Among others linguistic, mathematic-logical or musical intelligences are counted among them. (Gardner 2002, 69).

[2] See for example also books by Earley and Ang as well as Livermore.

also be, those who are interested will find references to the Bible in text boxes that I've inserted, and in the appendix.

I hope you'll enjoy making new discoveries!

Heike Tiedeck
August 2017

Chapter 1

Visitors to our home are normally astonished when they enter the living room, as they are met by a large African batik hanging on the wall, rattan furniture and colourful cushions next to typical German armchairs and seats. Gazing around, they will discover even more items from Africa: the wood carving on the wall, a game, a picture. We lived several years in Ghana and brought some of our household belongings from there to Germany because these things had become part of our lives. Every now and again we cook Ghanaian food – a feast for our son, who spent the first seven years of his life in Africa.

Tourists travelling to foreign countries are not only taken with the landscape and climate, architecture, music and writing, but are also fascinated with these things: the food, the objects of art and everyday use, as well as traditional costumes. Many people therefore enjoy encountering different cultures. But 'culture' means more than this. 'Culture' consists of different dimensions and, depending on which level the cross-cultural encounter takes place, it can turn out to be a stressful experience.

In this chapter the term 'culture' will be defined, and I will introduce you to the 'Onion model'. We will also answer the question: "What do an iceberg and 'culture' have in common?"

Definition of 'Culture'

The term 'culture' is derived from the Latin word *cultura* and signifies 'tilling', 'agriculture' and 'civilization'. In the wider sense of the word it denotes how people organise their social life and survival in a specific context and time. The anthropologist[3] Louis Luzbetak defines it as follows: 'Culture is a design for living. It is a plan according to which society adapts itself to its physical, social, and ideational environment… Cultures are but different answers to essentially the same human problems.'

A biblical perspective:

When God created man he gave him the task to work the earth and keep it (Gen 2:15), to fill it and subdue it (Gen 1: 28). This command is also called the "cultural mandate" that God gave mankind.

---

[3] Luzbetak 1963, 60–61 cited in Hesselgrave 1991, 100.

It is obvious that people in Greenland will need different clothes and housing than people in Africa. Finding and providing food in a desert or in a forest will be based on different techniques. So, the environment is a big factor in the survival strategy, that is, the culture.

In our minds we are now going to go on a journey to get a better understanding of what culture is.

The Onion – a Model

Imagine:

You've just flown into a country you've never been to before. You are now sitting on an air-conditioned bus from the airport to the hotel. Through the closed window you observe … what?

Reflect for a moment or write down what you might see.

Maybe you thought of things like these: Dress, building styles and different types of buildings, common means of transport, use of space, (e.g. shacks next to shopping malls, streets crowded or empty), written language, nature, weather, advertisements, animals, places of worship, wealth/poverty, pollution, ethnicity, hair styles, types of shops, colours, activities.

At the hotel you get off the bus and check in. After some rest you decide to walk around the local market. What do you notice?

Really give it a moment of thought before you continue reading.

Here are some examples: Smells, noise, language, music, how close people get to one another in encounters, behaviour patterns, non-verbal communication, interaction between different genders, bargaining, products, degrees of busyness, hygiene standards, decorations, containers for carrying, reaction to foreigners, currency, sense of pace, …

After a few days in the hotel you have the opportunity to stay with a local family for a week. Whilst you've enjoyed staying in the country up until this point, you now begin to experience some stress, even though the family is being very nice to you. You begin to be irritable. When you meet others from your group, you find that they've experienced the same. What is happening?

Try to put yourself into that situation.

You're experiencing culture shock. The everyday routine is unusual for you and you cannot always understand why people do what they do. How, when and what they cook and eat, how they visit each other, raise their children, rest, work, clean, their concept of hygiene, gender and age relationships, how important it is to fulfil one's task or rather invest in relationships, whether direct or indirect communication is used – all of this and possibly much more will be very strange to you. The difference in cultural values, as they are lived out in everyday life, causes stress.

While in the country you noticed the outer symbols of culture – the material culture, language – oral and written. You observed cultural behaviour. You were confronted with different values and different cultural rules in the family. Your visit in this country is too short to understand the deeper motives. What do people consider to be wrong, correct or desirable? How do they make decisions? What is the significance of religious places? What is true?

At the heart of this there are some basic assumptions about human existence: the worldview in its actual sense, which is even harder to grasp. It includes assumptions about powerful entities that are thought to be responsible for causing events in life, like God, angels, or spirits. It differentiates between the seen and unseen world, defines what is real and what gives meaning to our human existence.

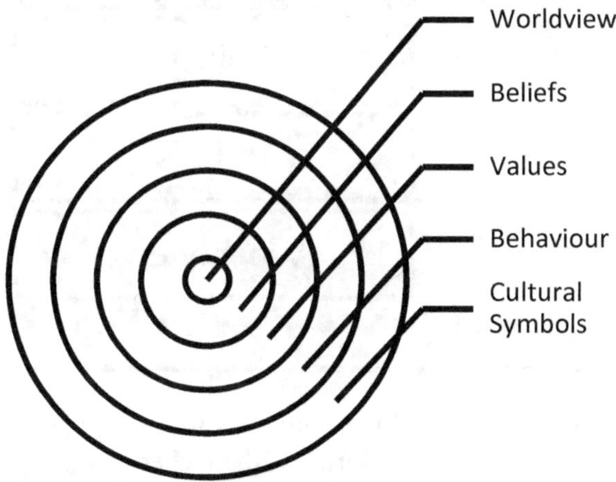

Culture can therefore be likened to an onion with many layers.[4] The deeper layers give meaning to the outer ones. (For both onion and culture, the following can be true: The more you peel – the deeper you get into it, the more you cry.)

---

[4]   Following Kwast in Winter and Hawthorne 1981, 361–364.

The Iceberg – a Model[5]

As we have seen, culture has different dimensions that are connected with one another. Instead of using concentric circles – as seen in the Onion model above – we can imagine them also as one being piled on top of the other, with worldview providing the foundation and cultural symbols (introduced, as the outer layer of the onion) forming the top. Taking a closer look at this Iceberg model, we see that only the top two layers are visible from the outside. For the other dimensions we can only draw conclusions indirectly from the behaviour of the people and their cultural symbols (like language, script, music, utensils).

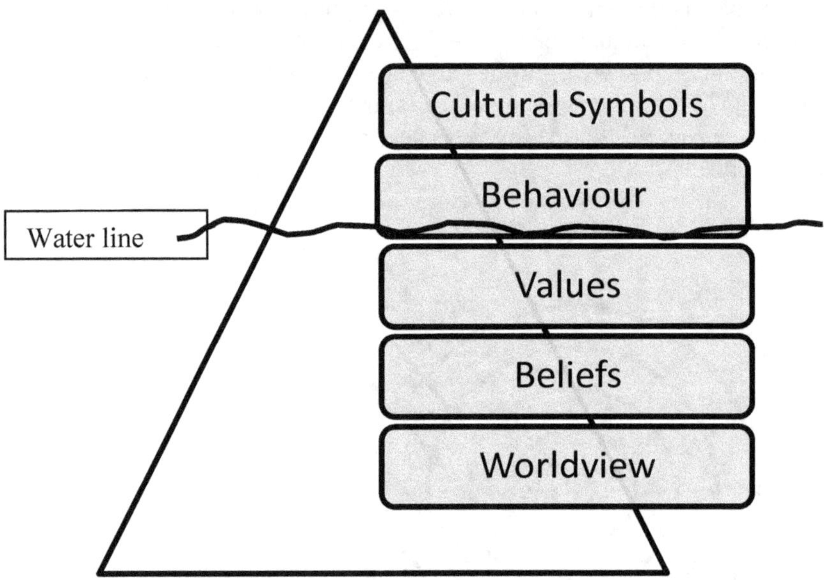

Cultural anthropologists therefore liken culture to an iceberg: only a small part is visible, or "external", with the majority of the iceberg remaining invisible, or "internal". Not only does this mean that a visitor to a new culture will be unable to access these unseen dimensions, but also the local person who lives in it is unaware of them. Just as a fish only wakes up to the reality of water when it is no longer there,[6] so we, too, become conscious of our own "internal" cultural imprint when we come into contact with a different culture. Worldview, beliefs like religion or ideology, and values are 'caught' rather than taught during childhood in the family or through kindergarten and school. They form the invisible part of culture.

---

[5]   Hall 1976.

[6]   Trompenaars/Hampden-Turner 1998, cited in Meyer 2015, 259.

Worldview

A worldview is a reflection of the way we perceive the world. It gives answers to questions like: "Is there a God? If so, is it only one or many gods? Is this god a person or an impersonal power? Is it present in all things or different and set apart from this world? How can I find a purpose in life? Is there a purpose? What is the fundamental problem of mankind? How can it be solved? What directs my decisions?"

When we put these questions before people, they will find some easy enough to answer, but with others they may find it hard to verbalise what they think or what drives them. Even though they are not able to frame their worldview in words, it still channels their thoughts and influences the other dimensions. For example, the Ebola crisis which hit West Africa between 2014 and 2016, can be interpreted against the backdrop of a folk-religious worldview, which would see witchcraft and curses as the cause of the epidemic that cost many lives. On the other hand, a scientific worldview would hold viruses and lack of hygiene responsible. In a similar way, jewellery is not necessarily just an expression of the material culture but can be worn as an amulet, that is, for spiritual protection. It is important to know that things and behavioural patterns can have a very different meaning from what we may assume because the underlying worldview is different from our own.

A biblical perspective:

In regard to "amulets": So Jacob said to his household and to all who were with him, "Put away the foreign gods that are among you and purify yourselves and change your garments. ... " So they gave to Jacob all the foreign gods that they had, and the rings that were in their ears. Jacob hid them under the terebinth tree that was near Shechem. (Gen 35:2+4)

Summary

- Culture can be defined as a strategy that shapes human existence.

- Culture has different dimensions, of which the majority are invisible and unconscious. The dimensions are connected with each other.

  - Conscious/visible culture: language, greetings, food, art, music, clothes, rituals, festivals, flags, games, jewellery, hairstyle, tattoos, piercings, and more.

    o   Unconscious/invisible culture: worldview, religion, spiritual convictions, decision making processes, power, respect for authorities, concept of time, identity, concept of justice, status, expressions of emotions (or the lack of it), logic, thought processes, understanding of cleanliness, child raising, ways of problem solving, expectation, assumption, and many more.

Intercultural Exercise

The following exercise can be used as an ice-breaker in an intercultural group:[7]

- Draw a basic outline of yourself.

- In the space surrounding yourself, write what people can observe or easily find out about you: Language, nationality or ethnic group, gender, age, religion, profession, hobbies, etc.

- Now inside the outline, write values and faith convictions that others cannot see or know unless they get to know you on a deeper level.

- Talk about your drawings in culturally mixed groups.

---

[7] This exercise draws from the "cultural x-rays". From IB Culture of Learning Conference in Madrid, 4–7 Oct 2012, about Third Culture Kids. http://www.ibo.org/contentassets/b53fa69a03d643b1a739d30543ca8d65/yoncaoktayma-drid.pdf (06.01.2017).

Chapter 2

We do it *this* way. How about you?

I visited a friend in the Philippines once and noticed her domestic help doing the dishes. I remember itching to challenge her way of cleaning. She used much too much soap on the sponge! She'd lather everything in soap while the tap was still running and then rinse it under *cold* water.

I was convinced of the German way of doing the dishes as the only correct way. That means warm water in a bowl, a measured amount of soap – considering the environment – and rinsing with hot water. So, I felt that I had to teach her how to do it in the only correct German way.

Do you recognize yourself in my behaviour? That you feel the urgent need to show someone else how to do this "in the correct way"? This does not happen in every instance in which we encounter difference, but with those that are important to us.

I had to reflect about my reaction in order to be able to understand it. My stress reaction was caused by the following (unconscious) thoughts: "She has to close the tap! She's wasting water and polluting the environment with all that soap!" Why did I react so strongly? When I was a child my parents did not have much money. We were taught not to waste anything. We were told off when we left the lights on or kept the tap running. In my youth the ecological awareness was formed: acid rain destroyed the forests in Scandinavia, and clean drinking water on the globe is scarce. These values of saving money and of environmental protection were deeply engrained in me, so much so that I got highly stressed when someone did not adhere to these values – to the point that I felt I had to make sure this domestic help would change her behaviour.

What about you? Do you recognize similar strong characteristics in yourself? Have you ever wondered where they came from? What about eating habits? How did your parents or others react when you did not do what was expected?

The above example shows how our upbringing influences our values, our behaviour and emotional reactions. While I was guided by the values of saving and environmental protection, the Filipino woman was concerned with the question of cleanliness. But for me, too, this was important as I thought that hot water killed germs and removed grease.

When cultural identity becomes the foundation of our judgements of each other we speak of **ethnocentrism**.[8] The underlying thought is: "How we do it is the best and only correct way. We are the best." You will find that most people groups and cultures have this attitude. Racism is a highly destructive form of ethnocentrism.

In order to be able to come together with people of other cultures, it is necessary to move out of the centre of our own universe and to be prepared to see the world through their eyes, to become **"ethno-relative"**.[9]

> *A biblical perspective:*
>
> *The Bible approves of ethnic identity. This becomes clear in a vision in which the Apostle John describes how people from every ethnic group will worship God together in front of God's heavenly throne (Revelation 7:9). The Apostle Paul stresses that through the death of Christ and in fellowship with Jesus the hostility between ethnic groups that functions as a dividing wall, has been overcome. (Ephesians 2:14)*

Since then I have learnt that many Asians find it disgusting to wash dirty dishes in a bowl, i.e. in dirty water rather than under running (and therefore fresh) water. In their eyes it can't possibly get clean in a bowl. A Japanese lady explained to other Asians: "The people in the West only imagine that the dishes get clean this way." Asians may feel uncomfortable if they need to eat from plates that, in their understanding, are not clean.

Cultural behaviour therefore contains an inner logic, at least for those who act according to it. If we want to be able to understand each other, it will be helpful to understand each other's logic. Moreover, it is important that we understand our own cultural background, as it forms the foundation for our emotional reactions to the differences that we come across in intercultural encounters.

For intercultural encounters to go well for us, we need to allow different life strategies, even if we find them strange in the beginning. We can assume that they are meaningful in the places where the people come from. When we move

---

[8]　"Ethnicity" on the other hand, describes a positive cultural understanding of oneself that has no intention of raising itself above people with other cultural identities.

[9]　In a short fable the author Duane Elmer (2006, 27) shows what can happen when we perceive the world only through our own "cultural spectacles": A monkey observes a fish struggling against the current. Full of compassion the monkey "saves" it. When the fish eventually stops flapping around on the dry ground his "saviour" is full of joy about the successful operation.

house we do not automatically change our behaviour. We take our life strategies with us. Yet we may find that they do not work equally well in every place we go to. This is what every immigrant will experience, especially when the first misunderstandings have occurred. A simple, yet helpful strategy for a conversation about each other's cultures could be the following sentence: "We do it *this* way. How about you?"

Summary

- An ethnocentric person claims: "Our way is best". Or: "Only this way is the correct way to do it."

- An ethno-relative attitude pre-supposes: "Different is not better or worse – it simply is different."[10]

- For intercultural encounters, it is helpful to first of all reflect and understand one's own cultural background and then to gain knowledge about other cultures.

---

[10] The statement has to be taken with care. But the basic attitude of ethnorelativism creates an openness and respect for difference.

Chapter 3

Common Ground – Foundation for Relationships

When I was 19 years old, I lived and worked as an au-pair, staying with a French family in a Parisian suburb. With the family there was also a young Portuguese woman. We became friends and eventually I visited her family in the north of Portugal. She came from a small farm without electricity or running water. I found it amazing that we – despite tremendous differences in family background and language – were able to understand each other on a deeper level.

Many years later I became a mentor for a Korean student. We talked about very deep and personal issues. At the end of her studies she said that she would never have thought, that she would be able to talk with a non-Korean about such private things. Her expectations in the mentoring relationship had not been very high because she was very conscious of the cultural gap between us.

What is it that all of mankind share in? Before we deal with cultural differences, let's have a look at what is common ground, no matter the cultural background.

> *A biblical perspective:*
>
> *Each person carries a print of God's image (Gen. 1:27) which has been distorted or distroyed by our broken relationship with God, by circumstances, other people or our own decisions. When cultural difference creates boundaries, the thought that all people on this planet share in the image of God can help make a connection to the other person.*

Ruth van Reken and Barbara H. Knuckles[11] remind us that we need to turn over the cultural iceberg when we want to build a bridge to another person, for underneath all the differences that we perceive, there is a person who needs other people, who wants to be respected and who longs for proof that he or she is significant. These are the fundamental needs of each person: relationship, respect and significance. Instead of becoming paralyzed with fear of making mistakes in intercultural encounters, we could ask ourselves: "Who is this person in front of me? How can I make contact?" That requires courage.

This would be similar to the following experience: maybe you were invited to a party, but you did not know any of the other guests. You felt lonely and

---

[11] Pollock and van Reken 2009, 234.

strange. While there are some who are content not to be bothered by others, maybe you belong to those who are delighted when someone approaches you to start a conversation. In a similar way, this is how many migrants feel in our midst.

Anthropologists[12] listed the basic needs which are common to all mankind in addition to those mentioned above. They only differ in the way these needs are met – depending on the culture. One basic need would be obtaining food. Whether one bakes loaves of bread or unleavened bread or eats rice three times a day or something completely different, whether you add butter or oil – this can vary. Further basic needs would be providing shelter, family, protection against external threats, education, and maintenance of the social system, transcendence and spirituality.

People who are committed to help refugees are active in these areas in order to help the newcomers fulfil their basic needs in the new environment. Conflicts arise where different social forms meet or where religions and values are so different that they no longer serve to integrate one another.

Summary

- Despite great cultural differences, intercultural encounters are possible because **all people have a longing for relationships, for respect and significance** and because they have the same basic needs.

---

[12]   For example Malinowski 1975.

Chapter 4

The Rules of the Game

When we returned from Ghana to Germany our seven-year-old son had to find his way in the German primary school culture. One day he came home and said: "Mum, there are so many rules I do not know." He did not refer to the rules at the school, but to those of the interaction among the children. With this he had defined an important part of culture: the rules of social interaction.

Our son had attended a Ghanaian kindergarten and an international school and had also experienced home schooling. It was not as such that "school" was difficult, but the completely different cultural orientation of the children. Why was this?

There was a fundamental difference: that German children focus on the *ME* while Ghanaian children think from the perspective of, *US*. A German child finds their identity in and through individuality; a Ghanaian finds their identity as part of the group. Me- and Us-Cultures[13] employ, in many ways, opposite rules of social interaction. If we focus on these, culture can be defined by Geert Hofstede in the following way:

"Culture consists of the unwritten rules of the social game."[14]

What are you supposed to do and how? What kind of behaviour is desired and what will be ostracized? Geert Hofstede found through international research that statistically, there are six independent cultural dimensions:

a. *Individualism/Collectivism* (Me-/Us-Cultures)
b. *Power distance* (steep and flat hierarchies)
c. *Masculinity/femininity* (focus on competition or on relationships)
d. *Uncertainty avoidance* (the ability to tolerate ambiguity or not)
e. *long-term/short-term orientation* (pragmatic or traditional ways of dealing with change)
f. *Restraint/Indulgence* (strict societal norms or free gratification of human drives).[15]

---

[13] See also Mühlan 2016, 15.
[14] Hofstede and Hofstede 2005, 4.
[15] Telelangue 2011, cf. Map-Consult n.d., Hofstede n.d.

A short quiz may help you to connect the theory with real life. Try to match those six dimensions to the examples listed below. You will find the solution at the end of the quiz.

1. Strict Muslims consider Western TV *Haram* (taboo).

2. On a hike in an Asian country, one of the walkers gets hurt. Some of the Western hikers decide to leave the group and to go ahead to get help more quickly. When they all meet again in the evening, it becomes clear that the local people were not happy with the decision of the Western visitors to leave the group.

3. In March 2015 a German pilot intentionally crashed a plane in order to commit suicide. Many people, i.e. everyone on the plane, died with him. As a consequence, the German authorities created more rules and laws to prevent such undertakings in the future.

4. Our son grew up in Ghana and absorbed many cultural clues. One of them was: do not look into the eyes of grown-ups. That was a sign of respect.

5. Territorial conflicts about the Åland and Falkland Islands were solved in different ways. The Åland crisis came to an end through negotiations and compromise between Finland and Sweden,[16] while the Falkland crisis resulted in a war between Great Britain and Argentina.

6. It is said that some East Asian countries have undergone rapid economic growth[17] because thrift and education are highly valued among their people.

The solution of the quiz: 1f, 2a, 3d, 4b, 5c, 6e.

Of all the above-mentioned cultural dimensions, the Me-/Us-Culture dimension (individualism/collectivism) is responsible for most cultural differences. One author therefore places this dimension in the realm of worldview rather than values.[18]

In the following section the differences between Me- and Us-Cultures will be discussed further.

---

[16] Jahn 2014, 2.

[17] Hofstede 2005, 210.

[18] Mühlan 2016, 45.

Me-Cultures

In Me-Cultures children are perceived as autonomous persons and affirmed in their individuality by involving them in decisions, giving them choice and fostering their strengths. Depending on how structured the culture is, the child will learn to follow rules or to do whatever they think is right. Personal responsibility and independence are the goals of their upbringing. The German culture is an example of a Me-Culture – as are the British and many other Western cultures. But in rural areas one still often finds a great sense of community, and people identify with their town, area or even with a club.

> *A biblical perspective:*
>
> *Aspects of Me-Cultures in the Bible: "making the best use of the **time**" (Ephesians 5:16). "But all things should be done decently and **in order**."(1 Cor. 14:40) "For we must all appear before the judgment seat of Christ, so that **each one** may receive ..." (2 Cor. 5:10). "Let what you say be simply '**Yes' or 'No'**;" (Matthew 5:37). "You are the God who sees **me**," (Genesis 16:13 NIV). "For whoever keeps the whole law but fails in one point has become **guilty** of all of it." (James 2:10)*

"***Ordnung*** muss sein!", "There has to be **order!**" This German saying shows that this society has rules which need to be kept by everyone. Whosoever does not will be punished.

Society is also structured by hierarchy, e.g. between a boss and the employees. In former times people like teachers, ministers and policemen were to be respected. Since 1968 when a student revolt challenged middle-class values many things have changed, also in the area of respect. When we returned to Germany from Ghana in 2004, I was surprised to be addressed by small children by my first name without any title of respect, like "Auntie" or "Mrs Tiedeck". Equality between the generations and also between the sexes has become more and more the norm.

'*Time*' is important. In Germany, nearly every household keeps a diary to keep track of appointments that give structure to life. Appointments are considered to be points of time. Punctuality is required.[19] Work and tasks give significance. That is why Germans are often preoccupied with the task at hand. Migrants quickly learn that people in this country have "no time" and that a visit needs to be arranged beforehand.

---

[19] In German punctuality is translated as *Pünkt-lichkeit.* The German word for point = Punkt is contained in it.

Truth: There's a saying in German: "Folks won't trust you anymore, because you've told them lies before". 'Truth' – in a German context – is usually expressed through words. Germans are mostly direct when they communicate; they mean what they say, and they say what they mean. If what you mean doesn't match what you say (in other words, if it's not literal), then it's viewed as being dishonest. In other cultures this may not be the case; often *indirect communication* is accompanied with body language. We once knew a Korean woman, who had never been to the Netherlands before. When she started out, she tried to find out what people were trying to express by interpreting their body language, rather than what they were saying. After a while she realised that in most cases, there was no hidden message to be found.

'Decisions' are made independently but are still often influenced by the guidelines of certain societal systems (e.g. you can't study any subject at university if you don't meet the prerequisites for the course.)

Us-Cultures

The majority of all cultures are Us-Cultures. The identity of the individual is defined by who you belong to: the family, the clan or the ethnic group. An African lady in Germany said: "Without family you are nothing." In many Us-Cultures nephews and nieces will be called sons and daughters; cousins, brothers and sisters; uncles and aunts are considered fathers and mothers. Children

> *A biblical perspective:*
>
> *Aspects of Us-Cultures in the Bible: "Welcome one another" (Romans 15:7). "... forgiving each other" (Colossians 3:13). "Count others more significant than yourselves" (Philippians 2,3). "Love one another with brotherly affection. Outdo one another in showing honour." (Romans 12:10)*
>
> *The Church of God has a 'one another'-culture. In it, every member is cared for (1 Timothy 5:8). Respect and esteem are also important values: "Honour everyone" (1 Peter 2:17).*

are raised to protect the name of the family or to make it greater. Often the family decides on the career a young person is to take, especially if it means an increase in the status, even if this path is not according to their own preference. The same is true in regard to marriages. The individual acts in accordance with the expectations of the group. Loyalty binds it together and gives protection to the individual. Children are wrapped in this sense of security that the family gives. Often, they are up till late into the night with the adults. No-one is left alone. Eating together strengthens friendships and trust. Here's an example: A group of Asian and Latin-American people travelled to a meeting from Singapore and Britain. Apart from me, all of them came from Us-Cultures. While I prefer to withdraw after a long journey to take a rest, this group was very happy to be invited to a barbecue. Despite their tiredness they preferred to be among other people rather than be alone.

Us-Cultures aim for harmony in relationships. This value is so strong that people would use "white lies" (half-truths) rather than destroy the peace. People are conscious of the fact that the wrong action on their part might cause the other person to lose face and to feel shame. Communication is therefore indirect. The actual words are not so important, rather people are used to reading between the lines. Non-verbal communication plays an important role.

Groups have a net of relationships. It may be that it is not so important *what* but *who* one knows. This "social capital" can be made use of in times of need.

As a rule, relationships and experiences are more important in Us-Cultures than schedules. If a particular moment is "just ever so pleasant" or if someone comes to visit, an appointment may be spontaneously cancelled (or missed). A Kenyan colleague pointed out the great difference between busy working days in the city of Nairobi and the unhurried leisurely pace of weekends. 'Time' is generally understood to be a broad space, rather than a fixed point, and so events and appointments could be understood much more flexibly. In some cases, punctuality – in the German sense of the word – can be considered rude. Those who are elderly aren't expected to rush or run about. They move at a leisurely pace which reflects their respected position in society.

After two years of studying at an intercultural college in Europe, a Korean student told us: "I still can't tell the difference between individualism and egotism." There will probably be many from strongly group-orientated cultures who think the same as she does. This indicates a mutual lack of understanding between Me- and Us-Cultures.

The difference between Me- and Us-Cultures can also be characterised by the contrast between 'hot-climate' (relationship-based) and 'cold-climate' (task-oriented) cultures, which refers back to observations made by US-President Thomas Jefferson. In a letter to Marquis de Chastellux in 1785, he wrote down his thoughts about the differences between people living in the northern and southern states: "These characteristics grow weaker and weaker by gradation from North to South and South to North, insomuch that an observing traveller, without the aid of the quadrant, may always know his latitude by the character of the people among whom he finds himself."

Dividing cultures into 'hot-climate' and 'cold-climate' groups requires all the cultures in the same climate zone to be similar. That's not quite the case. For example, China has a mostly temperate climate, but it possesses the qualities of 'hot-climate' cultures. Therefore, a distinction between Me- and Us-Cultures is more accurate.

Summary: Me- and Us-Cultures[20]

Me-Cultures	Us-Cultures
Identity in the Self	Identity in the Group
Justice-guilt conscience	Honour-shame conscience
Time/Task orientation	Event/Relationship orientation
Individual decisions	Group decisions
Development of an inner authority as means of control	The social group becomes the external authority
Appointment as a point in time	Appointment as a time span
Nuclear family, privacy	Extended family, little privacy
Direct communication	Indirect communication
Universalism: the rules apply to all	Particularism: Different rules for those belonging to the group and those outside of it
Egalitarian in regard to sexes	Division of gender and roles
Relationships in work and leisure activities	Relationships in the extended family

---

[20] Cf. Mühlan 2016, 29.

Reflection task:

Looking at the above list, what are you impressed about in regard to Us-Cultures? What can you learn from them? What do you value in regard to Me-Cultures?

Children of migrants[21] – who come from Us-Cultures and grow up in Germany or other Western countries – may try to bridge the cultural gap by doing the splits: with one foot in the culture of their parents and the other in the culture of their host country. Many of them have difficulties finding their identity. What kind of problems and opportunities can accompany this double identity?

---

[21] Keep in mind that not all migrant children come from Us-Cultures. Many of them originate from our European neighbouring countries. They, too, go through cultural adaptation.

Chapter 5

When giving a lecture on 'Understanding Cultures', I asked who had the right to rear children or discipline them if they were behaving badly. I knew a saying from my time in Ghana: "It takes a village to raise a child." While participants from the Middle East agreed with this statement, German participants reacted strongly: "No one has the right to discipline my child but me."

As was explained in Chapter Two, our reactions to cultural differences reveal how we've been shaped by our own culture. Sheryl Silzer calls this "Culture-based Judging System" (CbJS), the cultural value system, that we were taught in childhood. Thoughts and sentences like "How can someone eat something like that?!" or "Typical, late again!" are expressions of the CbJS. We judge based on the premise, that others have to do everything the 'right way', namely in a way which is familiar to *us*. Referring back to the Onion and Iceberg models (p. 13–14) these judgements are made on the level of cultural values.

This chapter will lay out how the culture type we belong to is reflected in our own Culture-based Judging Systems.

The Culture-based Judging System

Cultural differences can be perceived and assessed from as young as childhood: an Australian girl might be amazed that a woman from the Netherlands may wear the same clothes for a few days. One time when a British family visited us in Germany, the daughter whispered to her mother, "They don't have a TV!"

For an Australian family it's clearly important to change your clothes every day: to wear the same thing, day after day, would be seen as very strange and thus, wrong. And for this British family the TV is often on throughout the day. The kids saw this difference with the German family as something very strange.

When people from Me- and Us-Cultures meet, their different values and rules of social interaction often come into conflict with one another.

People from Me-Cultures become frustrated or irritated when:

- someone tells them what to do
- social pressure is used to make them conform
- others use their things without asking
- borrowed things are not returned without the lender having to ask

- they are expected to show gratitude or to reciprocate (pay someone back) if they have been helped by them

In Me-Cultures it is generally acceptable to:

- confront someone in public and even go so far as to shame them
- avoid lending your own things to others, or to expect the loaned item back in perfect condition
- speak negatively about someone who bows to social pressure

People from Us-Cultures become frustrated or irritated when:

- people belonging to a group don't take responsibility for one another
- someone doesn't use social pressure (e.g. they speak negatively about you when you're absent in order to make you conform)
- people refuse to share their possessions
- an individual does something that negatively affects the group's reputation (loss of face)

Conversely, in Us-Cultures it's generally acceptable to:

- punish those who don't take responsibility for others in the group
- speak negatively about those who don't conform and even exclude them from the group
- take from others who don't freely share with the group[22]

The example of raising children at the beginning of this chapter shows that there are different definitions of 'yours and mine', which can quickly lead to conflict. In Me-Cultures, an imaginary circle can be drawn around an individual and maybe their closest relatives. If someone punishes a child without being part of this narrow circle, this is viewed as an infringement in the eyes of the parents.

In Us-Cultures, the circle is drawn around a much bigger group of people. In the centre is the extended family, clan or village. Therefore, the whole group also has the right to raise a child. The aim is for the child to grow up as a respectable member of the group who will not dishonour them. In Me-Cultures, upbringing is geared toward the individual; in Us-Cultures it's geared toward the group.

---

[22] The above-mentioned distinguishing features are from Silzer 2011, p. 56–57.

Here are two examples of how the Culture-based Judging System can be felt when there are differences between Me- and Us-Cultures.

1. At the end of a pleasant evening at an international college in Europe, an Asian woman felt agitated by the fact that everyone was standing around in small groups, rather than sitting in one big circle in which everyone could talk with each other. Her CbJS had been shaped by a strong collective culture. Because she didn't see this ideal realised in a group mostly informed by Me-Cultures, she felt uncomfortable and judged the other students negatively.

2. In the film "My Big Fat Greek Wedding" a nuclear American family encounters an extended Greek family for the first time. At the end of the day, the head of the Greek family comes to this conclusion: "This no work. They're different people. That family is like a piece of toast. No honey, no jam, just dry!"

Four different culture types

Though helpful, the distinction between Me- and Us-Cultures does not reflect reality in all its nuances, as the following example will demonstrate:

A mother once told me, that she had to have the same discussion with her daughter every week as to whether she'd go to gymnastics or not. "Why can't she just accept that's the way it is?" The mother maintains the rule that gymnastics is every Wednesday, while her daughter wants to decide whether she goes or not for herself. She wants to make the choice afresh each week; everything has to be negotiated again and again. Both mother and daughter live in a Me-Culture. As explained in Chapter Four, the German culture is changing. Certain rules, etiquettes and hierarchies still held society together after 1968 and gave it structure. Now, these values are mostly found in institutions and among the middle-aged and elderly. The younger generations are becoming increasingly more individualistic. They want to be able to make decisions for themselves and choose from various possibilities, rather than simply being told what to do. Thus, in Me-Cultures we can distinguish between institutionalizing and individuating cultures.

In a similar sense, there are two main types of Us-Cultures. Historically, the British noticed this during the colonialization of Africa. When they came to the Gold Coast, the southern regions became colonies and the northern regions became protectorates, which were governed by 'indirect rule' (as a colonial power, they ruled through existing chiefs). In order to cover all the tribes using this method, people groups with no recognisable leader were made subordinate to those who were ruled over by a king or chief. That has caused tensions in northern Ghana which exist to this day. In Ghana all the tribes are Us-Cultures, but in addition to those which are organised as chieftaincies with a strong hierarchy, there are also those which are loosely made up of clans and led by a council of elders.

These types of Us-Cultures, both hierarching and interrelating, can also be found in other places across the world.

The Mary Douglas Model

When we look at Me- and Us-Cultures side by side and subdivide them into those with strong or weak structures, we find the four types of cultures that we discovered in the last two examples. These are attributed to the British cultural anthropologist, Mary Douglas.

A culture in which there is little cohesion of the group and everyone is able to do as they like can be described as *individuating*. In its truest form it doesn't exist. That would be anarchy. Geert Hofstede found that with a rising national income, the individualisation of the social culture also increases.[23] Initially, this becomes noticeable with the younger generations.

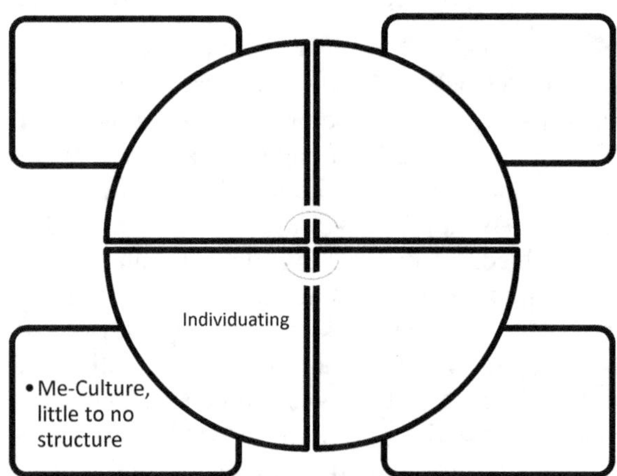

Diagram 1: Individuating

---

[23] Hofstede, 'Culture only exists by comparison'. https://geert-hofstede.com/natio nal-culture.html.

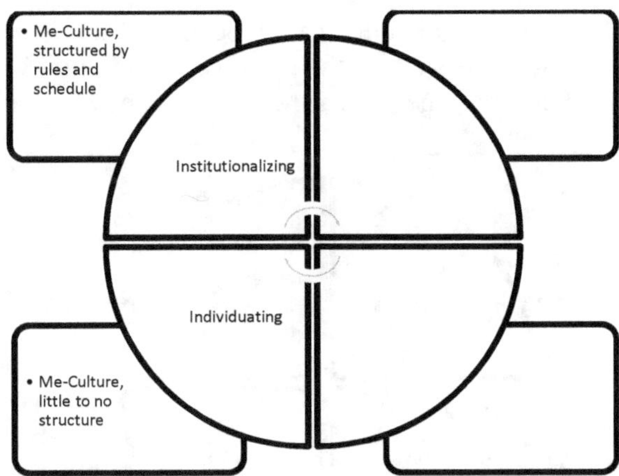

Diagram 2: Institutionalizing

Having little cohesion within the group, but structure in the way of rules and appointments, organisation and management – are the hallmarks of a culture which is *institutionalizing*. This is indeed how institutions function, but this also applies to some Northern European cultures, such as the Germans, Dutch, French, British, etc.

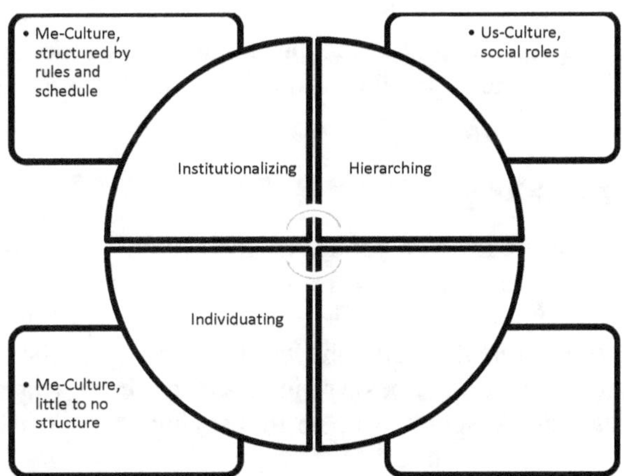

Diagram 3: Hierarching

"It's us against the rest of the world" could be considered as the motto of collectivist cultures. Being part of the group provides protection and requires loyalty. When there are distinctions between generations, gender, social status, and even the position in the age order of one's siblings, then a culture can be

considered *hierarching*. Social status can depend on one's ethnicity or cast, their skin colour, their profession, or their family's position or wealth. Hierarchies emerge in which everyone knows their role and place.

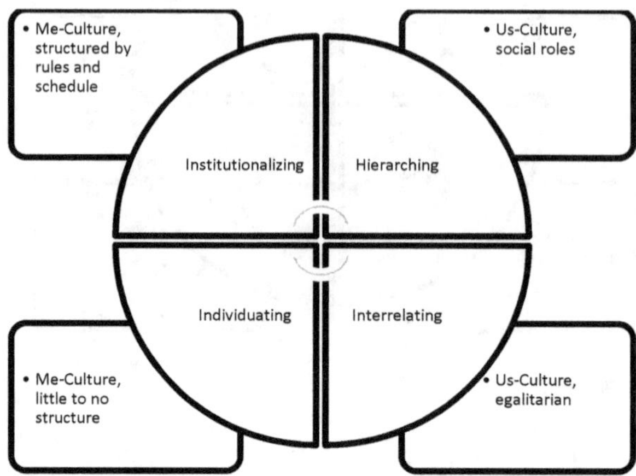

Diagram 4: Interrelating

When equality is emphasised in a culture and everyone is theoretically able to take on any position, then such a culture can be considered as *interrelating*.

The following paragraphs will describe these four culture types and their main features according to Mary Douglas, along with the specific CbJS for each one.[24]

Individuating Culture

An individuating culture is characterised by the need to bear personal responsibility and the possibility to choose from a number of options. Everything is subject to negotiation. Greed and pride can be the flipside of this way of life. It seems incomprehensible that someone would simply do as they've been told without question. If something goes wrong, it's "the others" who are to blame. The cultural ideal can be summed up in this saying: *"Rules are there to be broken."*

Institutionalizing Culture

Subordination to authority figures and compliance with rules are the characteristics of the institutionalizing culture. In some circumstances, injustice

---

[24]   Cf. Silzer 2011, p. 35–39.

within the system is tolerated in silence: *"There's nothing you can do about it. Rules are rules!"* People in this culture get irritated if someone refuses to abide by the rules (individuating), exerts social pressure (hierarching) or challenges authority figures (interrelating).

Hierarching Culture

Some Us-Cultures are characterised as strongly hierarchical. Respect is expressed differently, depending on the culture. Usually for important events, the programme only starts once the oldest or highest-ranking person has arrived. Everyone knows their place and how to behave toward others. I was told that when Koreans are unable to tell how to address their counterpart appropriately in their language,[25] they ask them what year they graduated from school or university in order to assess their age.

Networks and social connections are more important than rules. A lack of loyalty or respect puts the harmony of the group at risk or can be seen to be a source of harm, and (so it) must therefore be punished. A motto for this kind of culture would be: *"This is how things have always been done."* Authority figures have the power to exploit others. This is acceptable if they are materially better off. Great irritation is caused if the proper respect is not given to an authority figure (individuating), when support from outside the group is sought out (institutionalizing) or when someone challenges an authority figure because people within the group have been treated unequally (interrelating).

Interrelating Culture

The aim of an interrelating culture is to have equality in all spheres of life. *"The nail that stands proud is tapped down."* Those who belong to the group support each other with 'give' and 'take' in equal measure. Whosoever refuses to submit to the will of the group is excluded. Leadership is granted to influential characters who emphasise that they are part of the group. Decisions are reached by dialogue and consensus where possible. Inequality is quickly noticed and often leads to envy. It is expected that those who have more should share what they have and thus create balance and harmony. People belonging to this type of culture are irritated or baffled when people don't share or take more than others, when they make decisions only for themselves (individuating) or accept differences in status (as can sometimes be the case in institutionalizing or hierarching cultures).

---

[25]   As in many other languages, terms like "older brother" or "older sister" are used.

Summary

- The four culture types of the Mary Douglas Model differentiate between Me- and Us-Cultures and between 'strong' and 'weak' social structures.

- Our own cultural imprint is often felt to be "right".

- When a cultural ideal isn't realised, our Culture-based Judging System (CbJS) reacts with shock, stress or anger toward this "bad behaviour".

- Our CbJS is shaped by our upbringing. It is our reaction to other cultures and may indicate which cultural type we belong to. Relating to the Onion and Iceberg Models, these judgements are made on the basis of cultural values.

Intercultural Exercise

If you can think of an intercultural situation, in which you felt puzzled, irritated or stressed, take a moment to ask yourself the following questions:

- What happened exactly?

- What was my reaction, emotionally? What was it I reacted to?

- What values came into conflict?

- What can I learn about myself and my own cultural type?

- If you're reading this book in a group, exchange your answers with each other.

Chapter 6

In this chapter, see if you can identify the four different cultural types in the following examples.

Visit to Ireland

As a teenager I had pen-pals all over the world. When I turned eighteen, I bought myself a train ticket for the Easter holidays and travelled to Ireland to visit my pen-pal in Limerick. Since there was nobody to pick me up from the station, I took a taxi to get to the address I had been given. The driver asked me, "Are you sure this is the right address?" You could tell by the appearance of the street that it wasn't an affluent part of the city.

There was a lot for me to learn in the following week. I came from a typical, middle-class family in Germany, with my very own room back at home. Now I was in a family that had to make ends meet without a father. The mother lived with five children – some of them already adults – in a small house without a bathroom. It seemed obvious that I would be sharing a bed with one of the girls, but she had moved to share a bed with her mother. I found myself constantly surrounded by other people; there were also plenty of comings and goings with the neighbours. Even though everyone was very good to me, I was overwhelmed and very soon I wanted to go home. As a farewell gift I received a silver Claddagh ring, an Irish jumper and records with Irish folk music on them.

In the summer my pen pal came to visit us. Together with my sister we went on a round trip of Germany by train. When we had finished and were staying with my parents, she said, "Tell me, what do you think are the differences between our cultures?" I didn't give it much thought and said that they were the same. Of course, Ireland was not that far away from Germany, so why should the culture be any different? She said she found it strange that everyone in Germany lived behind closed doors. People didn't visit each other very much; everyone was more insular.

When I think about it nowadays, I'm ashamed when I think of the generosity I received from the Irish family.

If you want, you can think for a moment and consider which culture type I encountered at the time.

You would be right if you noticed that it was an Us-Culture. There was also no strong hierarchy, people shared what they had and they spent a lot of time with each other. It was, in fact, an interrelating culture. Having been a visitor in this instance, it's worth knowing that if you're presented with gifts, there is an expectation that you will eventually do likewise. It's not enough just to say, "Thank you."

Stress after a wedding

We were invited to a wedding in Ghana and for the drive home, we had arranged with some people from the church that they would be coming with us. Even though we'd already agreed how many people could come with us, that number still managed to grow! However, we had to make things difficult: the car only had five seats and even in Ghana it's not legally permitted to take more than that. The others thought: "No problem – everyone can just squeeze in!" The result was: stress and a bad mood in the car.

What do you think was causing this bad mood? What were the people thinking about each other? What does this say about their cultural type?

We were upset that our rule, 'no more than five people' wasn't being followed. This reaction clearly showed us to be people who had been shaped by an institutionalising culture, in which structure is created with rules and dates. Our passengers noticed our bad mood but couldn't understand it. How can a rule be more important than people, if everyone fits into the car anyway? They belonged to an Us-Culture (whether it was hierarching or interrelating can't be specified by this example).

In the Brazilian Rainforest[26]

An anthropologist and Bible translator lived with the Deni people in the Brazilian Rainforest. In order to shorten the week-long journey to where the tribe lived, an airstrip was built, which the locals were happy to help with. Problems arose when it came to the matter of payment. The anthropologist gave items to the chief that would serve as payment, expecting them to be distributed fairly. However, it wasn't long before some took whatever they wanted, leaving others with nothing or very little, and therefore dissatisfied.

What could the problem be here? What clues might we pick up on?

The white man assumed that the tribe was hierarching, that the chief had authority and would allot the communal work, that he knew how much each had worked and therefore how much each deserved to earn. However, the Deni were in fact individuating. Within the rules of their society, everybody did as they wished. The chief was more a head man who could make suggestions but

---

[26]   Example from Lingenfelter 1998, p. 65–66, p. 74–76.

effectively had no authority. Communal work only appeared when a piece of jungle needed to be cleared. Even then, each and every person decided how much work they wanted to do and how much of the land they were going to cultivate. In this example, they eventually found that the way to proceed best was to divide the work for the airstrip into sections. Every worker decided how many sections they wanted to do, and according to the amount of work they chose to do, the payment was negotiated with each individual worker.

En route

A culturally diverse group is travelling through Europe by train. Their cultural differences become clear when eating together. While others are still eating, one member of the group – having just finished – stands up and clears his plate from the table. The others protest: "We're still eating! Can't you wait until we're finished? How rude it is, that you would just get up and leave!" Shocked by this reproach, the quick eater asks: "What's the problem? I only went to clear my plate!"

Perhaps you hear yourself or your parents a little in this scenario. Which culture types do you think are colliding here?

For some, there are very clear rules of etiquette, which the fast eater was unaware of or had disregarded. These rules are the sign of an institutionalising culture, which has come into contact with someone from an individuating culture.

Life in Egypt

During my university year in England, I studied Arabic and Theology. Following this year, and as part of the programme, I attended an intensive Arabic course at a language school in Cairo. Together with a course mate, we looked for an apartment for two months. We found what we were looking for in a family house. The landlord lived below with his wife and adult unmarried daughter. As we moved in, he told us that he regarded us as his daughters, at which we were delighted.

At the beginning of our study, the school hosted a party which began at nine o'clock in the evening. We only needed to cross a wide street to get to the venue. The next day we received a visit from the landlord. He wanted to know where we were the night before. We explained it all to him, but from that point we knew that we were being watched.

Sometime later I received a phone call from a female teacher at the school. There were no mobile phones back then, so she called the landline of the family. The family in turn informed us that the phone call was for us, so that we would pick up the receiver in our flat. I spoke with her in English. No sooner had the call ended, the landlord came in again and asked how it was, that we were getting calls from an Egyptian man. I was bewildered. Apparently, the female teacher, who had a slightly deeper voice, had spoken in Arabic when she asked to speak to me. Since I – unlike my course mate – was not yet married at the time, he kept a closer eye on me.

The third instance led to tears. I had a friend in Cairo and wanted to visit her. To do that I had to ring her, but there was only one phone in the house she was in, and it was answered by the caretaker. I had to explain to him that I wanted to talk to said friend. As I returned from visiting her, I was chastized by the landlord. He had eavesdropped on my conversation with the caretaker and (again,) had drawn his own conclusions. As luck would have it, my friend rang again later that day and explained the whole situation. My reputation was saved.

Take a moment to consider which culture type I was dealing with. How can you tell which one it is?

In this example I was getting acquainted with a hierarching culture. The landlord was head of the household and was anxious to maintain the family's honour. The important thing was that the female members of the family gave no cause for shame. In order to integrate us into the existing social structure, we received 'daughter-status'. My course mate's husband was responsible for her, since she was already married. As for myself, the landlord took responsibility for me. In Egypt, Western women are generally said to be promiscuous. That's why he felt he had to take special care with me. Everything I did was viewed through this lens. His own unmarried daughter had a job but would live with her parents until she would be married. A woman must always be under the protection of a man.

Working Together

Some practical work has been assigned to an intercultural team. Two men are given the task of painting a room. Whilst one of them immediately starts dividing up the work and starts with his portion in order to do the job as quickly and as well as possible, the other one becomes increasingly dissatisfied. When they talk about it afterwards, it turns out they had completely different goals in mind. While the one was focused on the task at hand, the other wanted to get to know his colleague better by doing the work together.

Which one of the two men do you identify with? Which two culture types do you think are working together?

Here, a task/efficiency-oriented person meets a relationship/event-oriented person. This expresses the contrast between Me- and Us-Cultures.

An Indian in Sweden

As he met his soon-to-be Swedish father-in-law for the first time, the Indian bridegroom bows to touch the other's feet. With his hand still extended for a handshake, the older man thinks to himself, "Where did he go?"[27]

This little scene always makes me laugh. Which two culture types are meeting each other for the first time?

The Indian man comes from a hierarching background and naturally wants to show respect to the father of the family. In Sweden the opposite is emphasised: that all people are equal. It is therefore a Me-Culture with a strong tendency toward individualism.

Family Visits

Some of the Kosovan women had been coming to a German language course for years and began to complain when the new wave of Albanian, Kosovan and Macedonian refugees had reached its height in Germany. Those who had come to Germany years ago were settled. The new refugees came to 'visit' them. These 'visits' could be for a few days but could also extend to over a month. The visitors expected the family to provide hospitality, to make room for them and to share what they had. Culturally the family could not object, especially if the visitor was someone like the son of the husband's eldest brother. At this point they saw their culture as a burden, especially when compared to the German culture of visiting others.

What type of culture do you think is represented here? What might be the subtle clues?

In contrast to the German Me-Culture, the Kosovan-Albanian culture is an Us-Culture. The reference to the husband's family shows that there is a hierarchy that regulates how family members interact with each other.

> *A biblical perspective:*
>
> *The Bible doesn't favour any particular culture type. The good news of God's saving love can take hold in any culture. In fact, cultures change as a result of responding to the Gospel: forgiveness instead of vengeance; serving instead of ruling; taking responsibility for others, rather than only looking out for ourselves; and much more.*

---

[27]   Andersson 2016, 297.

Chapter 7

Causes of Cultural Misunderstandings

Cultural misunderstandings may arise from many things. A common thread may be that we don't understand the motivation behind certain behaviours or decisions. The following examples illustrate the point well.

- Mrs Müller does no laundry between Christmas and New Year's Eve, no matter how high the mountain of dirty clothes may become. She doesn't want to be held responsible if someone in the family dies at this time.

- A meeting on the bus: a man is on his way to work and sits next to a teenager, who has put his feet on the nice new upholstery. After some thought, the older man tries to persuade the teenager to behave by the rules. "You have your shoes on the seat!" was met with "Yeah. So?" The indication that his shoes could be contaminated by dog dirt and wouldn't be good for either the seat or the next passenger was also disregarded: "My shoes are clean." Still pressing on, in a low voice so as not to make a scene, the man asks, "Do you act like this when you're at home as well?" and receives the answer, "My parents are fine with it! Okay?" The man decides to take a drastic but effective measure. He speaks to the other passengers and says, "Take a look at this young man…" and already his feet are under the seat and stay there.[28]

- During my training as a nurse, I worked for a few weeks in ambulatory care: going on rounds to people's homes, sometimes to give injections or drop of medicine, other times for general care like helping people put on compression stockings. I loved doing this work and at the end of my time at the nurses' station, the team wanted to give me a little something to show their appreciation: one hundred deutschmarks – a significant amount of money at the time. The only problem was, the organisation didn't have any money designated for giving of gifts, so in order to have the money accounted for the sum of money was written up as some other expenditure. At first, I wasn't sure about the legality of it all, but I was calmed by the thought that the responsibility ultimately lay with the management and not with me. But still I felt uneasy on the inside. Before going to bed I opened my bible. Proverbs 16:8 caught my eye: *Better a little with righteousness than much gain with injustice.* (NIV) I was struck to the core. The next morning – a Saturday – I took the money, found the manager and gave it back. She didn't understand why, but I just had to do it.

What do these three stories tell you?

---

[28] Käser 2001, 94.

Cultural 'Operating Systems'

Like in computing, every culture has its own 'operating system', so to speak. Not every software can be used in any operating system and different smartphones have their own App Stores for their own configurations. So too, every culture has its own 'operating system', which is instilled in one's upbringing. Referring back to the Onion and Iceberg models (p. 13–14), this deals with the innermost level of a culture: the matter of worldview. The 'operating system' is that, which we know as our 'conscience': it knows what is culturally acceptable and what is forbidden, how one should feel if one has committed a transgression and what should be done to remedy it. It guides us to what is desirable (at least, from a societal standpoint,) and informs our motivations and decisions.

In the first place, 'conscience' has less to do with religion, and more to do with regulating social behaviour, which is conveyed through the traditions of society by punishing nonconformist behaviour in childhood. Conscience guarantees social cohesion.[29]

If a child has very few attachment figures, their conscience becomes predominantly guilt-orientated. If the parents often point out what "the others" will think, there is then a broader circle of reference, so their conscience becomes more honour-shame-orientated.[30] A fear-orientated conscience arises when one is threatened by things such as, "God is watching you!" or, "The ancestors are punishing you!" or even, "The Secret Service is listening in!"

Let's look at the three examples from the beginning of the chapter. Mrs Müller's conscience is determined by fear. She's superstitious and fears that someone in her family may die if she commits the 'taboo' of doing laundry between Christmas and New Year's Eve.

The man going to work on the bus tries to persuade the teenager to comply with social norms by appealing to his guilt-orientated conscience. When that proves to be fruitless, he brings in the other passengers. The young man fears public exposure and immediately reacts to the impending loss of face. His conscience is shaped by a shame-orientation.

The third example is a question of right and wrong in a normative sense. In this case, there's also a religious component to it. Although there was nothing to worry about on the interpersonal level – neither punishment nor exposure – God's word becomes the authority in this instance. The transgression was felt

---

[29]   Käser 2014a, p. 112.

[30]   Käser 2014a, p. 121.

in the form of guilt. Putting things to right cleared my conscience and brought a sense of relief.

Imagine that the operating system for every culture is like a particular colour, made by different quantities of the three primary colours. These three colours are the contrasting pairs, honour-shame, justice-guilt and power-fear.[31] These are fundamentally different orientations of life, deep in our cultural programming, which lead to misunderstandings and mutual judgement. The diagram below shows how cultures tend to focus on one of the three orientations, in which we think, feel and act.[32]

From a biblical perspective ...

... the conscience goes all the way back to the Fall. By eating the forbidden fruit, the close relationship with God was broken. The first people became aware of their nakedness (shame), they could differenciate good and bad (recognise guilt) and they began to fear God (Genesis 3).

In the next few chapters we will take a closer look at the three components of the cultural operating system.

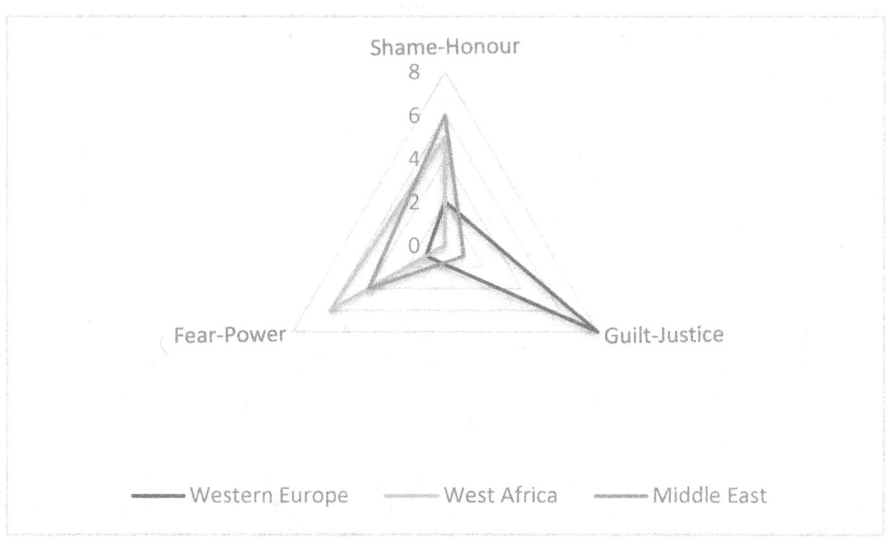

---

[31] Müller 2010, 112–117.

[32] You can test yourself on http://theculturetest.com/survey to find out how your own cultural operating system has been shaped.

Summary

- The human conscience acts like a (cultural) 'operating system'. In cultural anthropology a distinction is made between three components, which mostly appear together as a combination: honour-shame, justice-guilt and power-fear.

- These different orientations and their respective approaches to going about life often lead to misunderstandings and mutual judgement between those in an intercultural group, whether it be professional or social.

- In the Onion and Iceberg cultural models (p. 13–14) the 'operating system' would be at the innermost level of worldview.

Chapter 8

Every computer operating system requires a specific software, which tends to be incompatible with all others. When applied to cultures, we can recognise the operating system (comprised of the three orientations) as well as its corresponding 'software package'. In the Onion and Iceberg models, the 'software package' lies at the level of beliefs.

Honour and Shame

"Shame" here does not refer to psychological shame, but to a public disgrace, to being shunned, to the loss of reputation and face. As a Korean once said: "Shame means that you are finished."

The honour-shame conscience tends to develop where the opinion of the group determines who 'belongs'. Those who are 'in' have honour, and those who are 'out' experience shame and dishonour. Gossip and ostracism are a powerful and often unconscious means of bringing about conformity within the group. "What would the neighbours think?" is a classic thought which would govern behaviour. When misconduct is discovered, you're shamed. One tries to overcome this loss of face by restoring the honour that has been lost. It's important to know that this kind of reaction is only triggered when the particular offence has been exposed, i.e. made public. It can also be that the one who exposes the misconduct is seen as the 'real culprit', since they caused another to lose their reputation. Someone could also feel shamed, not because of their own bad behaviour, but because they were exposed by someone of lower status.[33] On the other hand, a person could be very pleased if they've succeeded in gaining an advantage without being

---

[33]   Cf Qureshi, 2014, p. 109.

caught.[34] When I tell stories in German lessons for migrants, the participants particularly enjoy it when the weak can outsmart the powerful.

The goal for the individual is to feel that they are an honourable member of the community. At the same time however, the behaviour of the individual always reflects back onto the group. When I asked a young Kurdish man what he did in his spare time, he answered that he spent most of his time at home. He was worried that people would talk about him if he admitted that he was meeting his friends. If someone in the Kurdish community started speaking negatively about his lifestyle, he would find it very hard to find a Kurdish wife. Apart from that, it would reflect badly on his family if he appeared to be out of the house too often.

Lost honour must be restored. This can be done by the disgraced person removing themselves from the group through suicide – especially in Japanese culture. Honour killings and terrorist attacks in Middle Eastern cultures would be a parallel.[35] Whoever restores the family or group honour in this way is often hailed as a hero.

For a long time, the honour-shame operating system played a considerable role in Germany as well. Wars were waged to restore the perceived loss of national honour. Young men were killed, all because they believed they were dishonoured and demanded to settle differences by duelling. In the end, it wasn't bans on duelling that brought change, rather it was that duels and wars were later frowned upon. Even in Germany today, a honour-shame culture still somewhat exists among young people. Social stock is put in being 'cool' or a sense of belonging to the cohort, such as the school class. In a honour-shame culture, the question: "Who am I?" is answered by those who influence the life of the individual. Relationships are crucial. That which is morally 'right' is defined as what would best serve the purposes of the community or a particular relationship. That which is 'wrong' would be anything that brings shame or disgrace.[36]

In the following paragraphs we shall look at some specific 'softwares' which can be run on the honour-shame operating system.

---

[34]   Cf Qureshi, 2014, p. 110.

[35]   Georges und Baker, 2016, p. 47.

[36]   Georges und Baker, 2016, p. 213.

Patronage[37]

Musah had borrowed some money from my husband, who waited for the agreed-upon repayment, but it never came. Instead, from the defaulting payee, he received an expensive traditional garment. My husband was bewildered and annoyed. And Musah's hopes for a further beneficial relationship were dashed.

Musah had acted in the spirit of the 'patron-client software' and tried to establish a relationship according to that notion. A patron-client relationship is the interaction between two unequal partners, in which the patron provides material goods, and as the counterbalance, the client 'repays' the patron with mostly immaterial things such as honour, thanks and loyalty. In the case of the expensive garment, Musah wanted to honour my husband and create a social debt on my husband's part to make sure that he would be there for him if Musah ever needed help in the future. By contrast, my husband wanted neither honour nor the role of a patron; he just wanted Musah to uphold his end of the agreement they had made. And since he didn't know much about cultures at that point in time, he couldn't recognise what Musah was trying to achieve with this gesture. The relationship broke down as a result of mutual misunderstanding.

We encountered this 'software' in another form when attending a harvest festival church service, in which a large collection was taken and that everybody there put into, by walking to the basket at the front. With each contribution, it was loudly announced how much each person had given. The more someone gave, the greater their reputation would be. We found it very uncomfortable, not only because there was an expectation on us to contribute, but also because we were used to giving anonymously. What we couldn't understand was that in the eyes of our Ghanaian fellow Christians, there was an invisible capital "P" (for Patron) written on our foreheads, whether we wanted it or not.[38]

> *A biblical perspective:*
>
> *When it comes to giving: "But when you give to the needy, do not let your left hand know what your right hand is doing, so that your giving may be in secret. And your Father who sees in secret will reward you." (Matthew 6:3-4).*

This kind of system actually works very well, when both parties accept and play by the rules. If this is not the case, it leads to a lot of misunderstandings. The rich, white Westerner, who is so *ungenerous* (or at least, appears to be so,)

---

[37] In the sense of a 'support system' between people of unequal means and status.

[38] Georges 2016b, Rich 2016.

is considered to be stingy, which is a terrible sin in most Us-Cultures, not just in Africa. On the other hand, people from Me-Cultures who work in Us-Cultures often complain about the financial dependency of the locals, or about corruption.[39]

> **What counts as 'corrupt'?** In the strictest sense, the word means 'rotten' or 'rancid'.
>
> In the context of Us-Cultures, it's considered corrupt when one doesn't give advantages to a member of their group, even though that person could.
>
> In the context of Me-Cultures, it's considered corrupt when one doesn't uphold "equality for all" and it is seen as unfair if one shows favouritism. It's considered reprehensible if advantages are given to some, and not others.

If you have grown up in a Western culture with very different social rules, how would you act in a culture that promotes the patronage system?

A young German, who had grown up in Latin America, found the patron-client system completely natural and emphasised that "If you want to have connections here, you have to be willing to adapt, because that's just how relationships work here."

Event and Relationship Orientation

I once met a migrant woman on the street. We greeted each other and exchanged a few words. As we departed, she began to run. She obviously had an appointment with somebody else that she had to make but hadn't let me know that. Her relation to me, and the fact that we met each other (the event) was more important to her than the appointment.

When someone from a relationship-oriented culture arrives late, they are often accused of being slow or unpunctual. On the other hand, if I only greeted someone from such a culture with a short 'hello' in order to be on time for an appointment, the other person may take it personally or feel rejected if they come from a honour-shame culture, because I didn't take the time to greet them properly. If, however, the other person shared my orientation toward punctuality, then they would be more likely to understand that I have a good reason to hurry.

In Ghana there would always be a long welcoming ceremony whenever a guest came over. Both sides would ask how the other slept, as well as about the wellbeing of all family members. Water would be brought in and then after

---

[39] Cf. Käser 2014a, p. 126.

having drunk it, the whole ceremony would begin all over again. If a guest had any concerns, it would mostly be discussed at the very end of the visit, almost before saying goodbye. In this way it was emphasised that the other person was more important than anything else. Of course, though, this approach was far from being time efficient.[40]

Indirect Communication

Since harmony and keeping face are so important in honour-shame cultures, communication is often indirect. Saying 'no' to someone's face is seen as an affront, especially if it's said to someone of higher status. Whether one's choice of words reflects the truth or not is not the important thing here, rather it's the intention to be polite, to keep the peace and maintain the honour of the other, which lay in the foreground. Westerners often condemn this kind of behaviour as untruthfulness, lying and fraud.

When it comes to resolving conflicts with indirect communication, an intermediary person is often called upon, with whom one can talk more openly, since the person is not personally involved. Because shame is such a strong emotion, it's common practice to allow some time for emotions to simmer down before resolving a personal conflict. Conflicts can also be resolved by non-verbal means, such as by giving a gift or an invitation to a meal together.

A biblical perspective:

Jesus tells a parable of two brothers who have been asked by their father to help in his vineyard. The first brother says, "I will not" but later changes his mind and goes to help after all. The second brother says, "Of course I will, father!" but then he doesn't. Which one did the will of his father?

One may wonder about this question, but for those who come from honour-shame cultures, it's understood that the second brother is actually honouring his father by saying "yes", even when he means "no". The first brother is insulting his father by saying "no" to his face. Jesus corrects this cultural norm by making it clear: it's not outward affirmation but the actual action that counts as obedience to the Father (Matthew 21:28-31) (cf. Hofstede 2005, 87)

---

[40]   Andrews 2015a.

Purity

Hygiene and religion are strongly linked in the minds of many people across the world. One only has to think of the ritual ablutions in Islam and Judaism. Someone who thinks of the left hand as unclean (since it was traditionally reserved for cleaning after using the toilet,) would be offended if they were given something with that hand. A left-handed Westerner or someone who washes their hands thoroughly wouldn't think anything of it and might not notice or understand the reaction from some others. Similarly, the footballer, Messi, angered the Egyptians when he gave away a pair of his football boots for auction on a television show in Egypt. As with many other cultures, in Egypt, shoes are "the epitome of impurity"[41] (This is why people take their shoes off when visiting peoples' homes in many parts of Asia. In Japan and Korea, people even have an extra pair of slippers for when they go to the toilet.)

Purity has a lot of meaning in honour-shame cultures. In Kurdish houses, for example, the floors are covered in white tiles and have to be cleaned frequently. In the Middle East, a man's honour, for instance, is closely intertwined with the moral purity of his female family members. In some African countries well-polished shoes – rather than flipflops – are worn to school, work or church, because clean shoes are thought to reflect an inner purity.

> *A biblical perspective:*
>
> *"Impurity" plays a large role in the Bible. It can be both a medical term as well as a social one, such as referring to those suffering from leprosy and being excluded from the local community. It can also be an expression which has to do with religious duties. Jesus gives "impurity" a new definition:*
>
> *"Do you not see that whatever goes into the mouth passes into the stomach and is expelled? But what comes out of the mouth proceeds from the heart, and this defiles a person. For out of the heart come evil thoughts, murder, adultery, sexual immorality, theft, false witness, slander. These are what defile a person. But to eat with unwashed hands does not defile anyone." (Matthew 15:17-20)*

---

[41] Blick 2016.

Hospitality

Whenever I visit our friends from the Middle East, at some point a bowl of fruit will be served and bite-sized pieces will be laid in front of me. In an unannounced visit to a Chechen family, there was so much food put on the table out of hospitality that it seemed the table would collapse under the weight of it. The question, "Can I offer you something?" was never asked. If it were, it could be understood as very rude.[42] Hospitality and generosity are a matter of honour. In Ghana, anyone who was having dinner when somebody came by would say "You are invited", even if there clearly wasn't enough to go around. It was then up to the invitee to work out whether it was just politeness or whether it was an actual invitation. If I wanted to make friends with a Chinese or a Brazilian, eating a meal together would be essential.

A biblical perspective:

Hospitality also plays an important role in the Bible: "Do not neglect to show hospitality to strangers, for thereby some have entertained angels unawares." (Hebrews 13:2)

In our time in Ghana, a local person once told me that he couldn't fathom why we, a family of three, would cook in such small quantities. What if a visitor suddenly came around? Our behaviour toward food and not wanting anything to go to waste made us seem self-centred. On the other hand, we found it hard to understand why families in Ghana would put themselves deep into debt so that they could finance celebrations, such as a naming ceremony for a newborn baby, or for a wedding or funeral.

Social Roles

When visiting the Philippines, I was asked some very personal questions, like "Are you married?" or "How old are you?" I could also have been asked about my income. Why all these questions?[43] In a hierarchical social structure, everybody has their place, and therefore it is important that people find out where they stand in relation to one another. Every time there's a newcomer, they have to be categorised. This also applies to linguistic subtleties. Which title or form

---

42   Andrews 2015b.

43   Andrews 2015a.

of address is right? An African friend of mine who lives here in Germany insists on calling me "Mrs Heike". Because I'm older than her, she has to pay me respect according to her own cultural understanding.[44]

For the Dagomba people in northern Ghana, respect is highly valued and is reflected through status. If we passed someone in the village who was older than us, we would bow as we walked. If we visited an elderly person in their house, we would squat in front of them without making eye contact, until they would clap their hands and we would be allowed to sit. When my parents came to visit us, we were invited to dinner by the family of our language assistant, and we were asked to bring filtered ice water with us. On the way into the village, my still very active father (who was sixty years old at the time,) carried the water container. When we entered the village, we passed by a group of men relaxing in the shade. Suddenly they became very restless and started calling me names. Why? As a woman – and a young woman at that – I should've been the one carrying the water. In their minds it was an unthinkable disgrace that an elderly father should have to do it. Trying to explain that it was very different in our culture didn't help at all.

In Northern Ghana, women are ranked lower than men, and when it comes to the men, the young are ranked below the old. There are clear hierarchies of power and of respect. On one occasion a girl in our neighbourhood was making fun of us because we weren't speaking her language properly. With my rudimentary language skills at the time, I put together the sentence "You're not paying me any respect." This was a serious accusation. The grandmother of the family then came out to apologise for her grandchild's poor behaviour.

With different status comes different roles: for the Dagomba people, men iron clothes and wash cars, while women cook meals and fetch water and firewood. In cities, however, these roles are slowly changing.

Are these roles and statuses unfair and oppressive? That depends on the point of view. A positive outcome of this system is protection for women when they are accompanied by male family members. One could also argue whether or not it is a loss for society as a whole, when external signs of respect no longer play a role.

Most cultures in the world are oriented around honour and shame. Many people from such cultures now live in Germany and other Western nations as well. It therefore makes sense to deal with the differences between our operating systems.

---

[44]   Andrews 2015b.

Chapter 9

Justice and Guilt

A small proportion of people on this planet belong to 'W.E.I.R.D.' cultures. Of course, I don't mean that these societies are unusual per se, but that they are Western, Educated, Industrialised, Rich and Democratic. In essense, this is generally descriptive of all Me-Cultures.[45] In 2010, three psychologists wrote an article, in which they made the case that psychological research is primarily conducted on individuals from W.E.I.R.D. cultures. They stated that only a small, unrepresentative snippet of humanity had been recorded and therefore, that the findings should not be generalised to all humankind, as had been the case so far.[46]

The conscience of an individual from a 'W.E.I.R.D.-Culture' is shaped by the notions of guilt and justice. Everything that happens falls into the moral categories of right and wrong. And when something is wrong, we look for the person who is responsible. In Us-/shame cultures, relationships are the focus of attention, and therefore people respond "to violations against norms considered generally accepted rules of *decency, propriety* and *civilised behaviour.*"[47] In Me-/guilt cultures, rules and laws inform the conscience of any trespass that would be called "sin" and so result in a bad conscience. Since personal liberty is emphasized in Me-Cultures, there is no strong pressure to conform to a par-

---

[45] Exceptions to this would be Southern European states, which although are W.E.I.R.D., are still Us-Cultures. Japan is E.E.I.R.D. (E for Eastern,) but is still very much an Us-and shame-orientated culture. One also supposes that the Four Asian Tiger States (South Korea, Taiwan, Singapore and Hong Kong) have also adopted elements of Me-Cultures as a result of globalisation. (Blog from Georges 2017a)

[46] Henrich, Heine and Norenzayan 2010.

[47] Käser 2014a, p. 116.

ticular group as with Us-Cultures. However, youth and village culture can display a strong shame orientation even within Me-Cultures, since the individual wants to be acknowledged by the group.[48]

Imagine the following Scenario:

> In school it's announced over the loudspeaker system, that "H." should make their way to the headmaster's office.

What do you think? What could the reason be?

In a justice-guilt culture,[49] the assumption is that H. has done something wrong and that a reprimand awaits him/her. In an honour-shame culture one would never expose someone in such a public way (i.e. over a loudspeaker,) and so the assumption is that he/she is receiving an award.

Here's another example:

A foreigner in the Philippines stops his car at the red traffic light while everyone else drives by. Content that he's abiding by the law, he leans back in his seat as the police officer knocks on his window and points out that he's obstructing traffic. Still, the foreigner is convinced that he's in the right. The conversation escalates and the officer confiscates his driving licence, though he's allowed to drive on. The next day, he goes to pick up his licence at the police station and finds out that he has to pay a fine first. Unaware of any wrongdoing, he initially refuses and insists on his rights, until he's advised by an officer to pay the fine – regardless if it's right or not – to get his license back and leave.[50]

Which side do you identify with? The foreigner or the police? Can you tell what's gone on here?

To 'insist on one's rights' and to demand justice according to the law is completely normal for our aforementioned foreigner, since it's how he's been culturally shaped. What he doesn't realise is that his actions at the traffic light (that is, insisting that he was right,) undermined the authority of the police officer. The whole process of confiscating the foreigner's licence and the administrative fine serve to restore the officer's honour.

Just as in the case of honour-shame, the justice-guilt 'operating system' also comes with its own special 'softwares',[51] which we will now examine.

---

[48]   Ibid, p. 153.

[49]   Some authors speak of 'innocence' rather than 'justice'.

[50]   Rose 2017, p. 5.

[51]   Georges and Baker 2016, p. 60.

Independence

An active, ninety-year-old German man still lives alone, even though he has the option of living with his son. He doesn't like people "mothering" him and loves his independence. By contrast, an old, Afghan lady lives with her daughter. For both women, it's completely normal that the daughter should look after her mother in her old age. The old woman is honoured by this relationship and it would be unthinkable to her to live alone.

We raised our son to be independent. My Latin-American friend finds it strange, that he left home "so soon" – after finishing school. In her understanding of these things, a family should live together for as long as possible.

From a certain age, our son received a monthly allowance (or 'pocket money' to our British friends) as well as his own bank account. With this, he should learn to handle money so that one day he would be able to do so independently. "An allowance? What for?" ask the parents from Us-Cultures. "Our child already receives everything they need from us!"

In Western culture, independence can also be embodied by thinking for oneself first, which also includes financial aspects. Many people from Us-Cultures – for whom generosity and 'interrelatedness' with others is very important – see this way of thinking as very cold and heartless.

Direct Communication

"State the facts!" – "Just say what you think!" A Dutch colleague of ours always did that; you always knew where you stood with him. If he was pleased with something, he would say. If he wasn't, he'd make it known just as much. It was clear to him that he was evaluating a thing or situation, not a person.

Having spent a long time working in the Netherlands, I've learnt that there are different levels of direct communication in Western culture. Here's a small example of it, played out by two students – one Dutch, the other Australian. At a group meeting, dried prunes are put out among other small snacks. The Australian student raises her eyebrows and says "Well, those are very high in fibre." The Dutch student responds: "Yeah, they really help you go to the toilet, don't they!"

Direct communication avoids frills and is very matter of fact. Using the right words is important, especially in things like agreements or contracts that have to be written down in exact terms. By getting straight to the point, you save time. The majority of people on this planet, however, just find this downright rude.

When it comes to conflict, it's generally recommended to have a one-on-one conversation, to state the facts as they are, and in so doing, arrive at a solution to the problem. If one person has done wrong to the other, then they're expected to acknowledge their fault and ask the other for forgiveness.

Task / Time Orientation (Efficiency)

Two staff members arrive at their open-plan workplace in Ghana; one is Ghanaian, the other is from a Western country. The Westerner comes in and scuttles quietly, trying not to disturb anyone. The Ghanaian, on the other hand, comes in and begins to go around greeting everyone with loud and lengthy conversation.

Efficiency and personal relationships often lie at opposite ends of the workplace spectrum. When a student once told me that she couldn't come to my class because her child was ill, I pointed out to her that that there was still content that would need to be covered. Only then did I think to ask what the matter with the child was and if she needed any help.

The separation of facts from people allows for efficiency – often at the cost of personal relationships.

Science / Secularism

A birthmark or strawberry mark on one's face may be seen as a harmless beauty mark in Western culture. The young daughter of an American family we knew in Ghana, proudly explained that she had "an angel's kiss". It was wise for the parents to give a positive, supernatural explanation for the mark, otherwise it could have been interpreted by local customs to be the result of evil forces at work. A purely scientific answer would have been of no use, either to the locals or to their daughter.

A biblical perspective:

The Bible differentiates between faith in God and superstition, e.g. in Colossians 2:16ff. The creation account already points out that stars are there to give light and orientation – which lines up with scientific findings (Their purpose is not for fortune-telling). (Gen 1:14-18)

In the eighteenth century the notion of truth had become scientifically redefined by the Age of Enlightenment. The world had been "de-spiritualised"; all causes and effects now had a scientific explanation. We have been shaped to think like that in the West. In many parts of the world people go to mediums and diviners to find out why someone has died. Instead of reacting to a pandemic with stronger hygiene measures, offerings are sometimes given to appease spiritual forces. However, there are also superstitions in Germany which exist alongside science. Why else would it bring bad luck if you tell somebody "happy birth-day" in advance, or crossing your hands over each other when shaking hand with multiple people, or come across a black cat?

Convenience / Functionality

In my husband's family as children, he and his siblings would find their Christmas presents under the Christmas tree, unwrapped, but covered by a blanket, from under which they would be brought out one by one. They didn't know any different and it saved on wrapping paper and the mess that would follow. Practical, useful and to-the-point: these are the values that were in the foreground.

For my Latin-American friend, something like that would be unthinkable. If she's organising something like a child's birthday, there's a certain amount of effort that goes into it naturally: there has to be a theme which informs everything in the party, from the cake to the decorations to the guests' costumes. In all respects, it has to be beautiful. There is no cost too great and no amount of effort to high, and if a "real" celebration is deemed impossible due to financial reasons, then it's better not to celebrate at all.

Egalitarian / Equality

When I was a child, the grown-ups in the kindergarten and friendly neighbours were greeted with "Auntie" or "Uncle". In Ghana, it was also customary for children in the international team to integrate the adult workers into the extended family circle and to refer to them as aunts and uncles. After we returned to Germany, we had to get used to the fact that titles of respect had mostly been done away with. Even our actual nephews and nieces didn't use them when talking to us.

While I had observed as a child in Germany, that my mother would sit in the back seat of the car if another man than my father was travelling with us, (and I had internalised this as a rule of common decency,) I learned from my Dutch colleagues in Ghana, that the wife would obviously sit in the front with her husband and the guest – no matter of their gender – would sit in the back.

These two examples show that Western culture is not standardised and that it has changed in many respects in recent years. Perhaps it's good to keep in mind, that treating others equally and the gradual withdrawal of preferential treatment and etiquette should not be misconstrued as signs of disrespect.[52]

---

[52] Lanier 2000, 92–93.

Chapter 10

Power and Fear[53]

In the background of this cultural 'operating system' there is a 'software', based on the notion that powerful entities must be satisfied. These entities can be spiritual beings or – often in the case of dictatorships – rulers who fill people's lives with fear. The actions of an individual in this setting are aimed at one of two goals: to gain power in order to determine the fortunes of themselves or others; or to manipulate or satisfy the powers one is under, in order that they may be benevolent toward them. In most fear cultures, the world is viewed as being inhabited by spirits, whose influence should either be feared or attempted to use to one's own advantage. In some cultures, this spirit world includes ancestors, whose influence is still seen as being influential. In turn, the ancestors' opinions of the life of their descendants is of great importance. In this worldview there is no distinction between the "natural" and the "supernatural", the material world exists alongside and is heavily influenced by the invisible world.[54]

> *A biblical perspective:*
>
> *The Good News for people with a conscience that reacts with fear: Jesus says: "Fear not, I am the first and the last, and the living one. I died, and behold I am alive forevermore, and I have the keys of Death and Hades. (Revelation 1:17-18)*

Manipulation

Rituals, amulets, taboos and acts of sacrifice are widespread, as well as the tendency to 'trick' the higher powers. Ronaldo Lidorio describes how, among the Konkomba people in Northern Ghana with the introduction of the new idol Grumadii into their tribal area, many animal sacrifices were required to satisfy this 'god': "At the birth of a child, the family would have to sacrifice an animal to *Grumadii*. By doing so, it would mean that *Grumadii* would now have power over the child by virtue of the name the child was given at birth. However, many feared the influence which *Grumadii* – the embodiment of evil – may exert on the new-born. So, people would try to trick him, by giving the child only a temporary name at birth, when the sacrifice would be given. It was believed that the greatest danger would be over after six months or so, and

---

then *Grumadii* would no longer be able to influence the child's soul with his evil."[55]

In German and English idioms we also use a sort of deception tactic: we wish someone well who is about to do something important (sports' match or theatre performance) by saying "Break a leg!" The thought behind this is that if evil forces hear that something bad has already been wished, they will no longer cause harm and will leave the person alone. It's in this same train of thought that we take an umbrella with us, "so that" it doesn't rain. Spitting over the shoulder, knocking on wood and wearing amulets: all these rituals and objects are intended to ward off evil spirits. As mentioned back in Chapter Seven, Mrs Müller leaves her laundry unwashed between Christmas and New Year, so that she doesn't break the taboo which could offend invisible forces. (p. 41)

> *A biblical perspective:*
>
> *The Old Testament tells the story of a power encounter between the Canaanite idol Baal and Yahweh, the God of Israel. The prophet Elijah meets with the priests of Baal on mount Karmel. The question is: Whose god is able to ignite the animal sacrifice without human help. The priests of Baal limp around the altar for hours, they cut themselves until blood gushes out and call their god making a lot of noise in the hope of convincing him to ignite the sacrifice. Elijah by contrast soaks the animal sacrifice in water, speaks a short prayer – in response to which God lets fire fall on the sacrifice. (1 Kings 18)*

Jealousy and the 'Evil Eye'

In many honour-shame cultures the power-fear aspect is also somewhat included. One is mindful of the *evil eye*, and so one avoids receiving compliments in order that they do not attract the attention of evil forces and shares (or hides) what one has so that the curse of envy doesn't come upon them. In such a culture, one would expect to find children being made to appear ugly, so that evil forces have no interest in them. For the same reason, parents will say derogatory things about their children and not praise them. Pieces of jewellery tend to be amulets in disguise and are intended to avert the *evil eye*.

---

[55]   Lidorio 2007, 21. (This episode cannot be found in the English version of the book.)

Power Words and Mana

Many people believe that negative words, especially when said in anger, can be interpreted as curses because words have a lot of influence, especially if they are spoken by someone with 'power'. In this case, 'power' is understood to be the ability to achieve things which are extraordinary.[56] So it's possible that nobody would tell a sick person that they were dying, out of fear that they would be held personally responsible for the death.

In general, it's desirable to increase one's own 'power', for example through rituals. In Ghana, children would often come to us to ask us for water. They would then go to the village and tell people, "We've just drunken water from the white people. That has a lot of *yaa* (power)!" The technical term for this lifeforce or power is *'mana'*, and it can also be encountered in the world of online gaming.

In the minds of the population, one can be 'infested' by bad mana through no fault of their own. This can have a negative effect on those around you and may lead to certain members of the community being accused of witchcraft. In Ghana there are entire villages of outcast women who have been branded as witches.

A biblical perspective:

Faith in the God of the Bible does not go together with occult practices. "There shall not be found among you anyone who burns his son or his daughter as an offering, anyone who practices divination or tells fortunes or interprets omens, or a sorcerer or a charmer or a medium or a necromancer or one who inquires of the dead, for whoever does these things is an abomination to the Lord. (Deuteronomy 18:10-12)

In Japan, drivers have their cars cleaned not only of dirt, but also of bad *Qi* as a form of spiritual car washing.[57] In this example, the connection between hygiene and spiritual powers is made particularly clear.

---

[56] Käser 2014b, 66ff.
[57] Lübbehausen 2014.

Dreams and Mediators

Dreams have great influence on people's lives. A dream can feel so real that, for example, a woman may separate from her husband because she had a dream about him having an affair.[58] Dreams are seen as a window into the invisible world, in which there is 'knowledge' that one needs so that they are able to live a successful life. There are also specialists (e.g. mediums or shamans) who can obtain this 'knowledge' via spiritual beings.[59]

A biblical perspective:

In the Bible, too, dreams play an important role. Joseph, husband to Mary, received instructions from God in a dream: He was not to leave his fiancé Mary, despite her pregnancy out of wedlock. He was even given the name of the child (Matthew 1:19-24). Later he was warned against the murderous intentions of King Herod and fled with his wife and son to Egypt. (Matthew 2:13-15)

---

[58]   Käser 2014b, 191.
[59]   More information can be found in Käser 2014b, 220–252.

Chapter 11

Intercultural Communication

We had only lived in Ghana for a short time when we were able to move into our little house. It was in a rural area. We were supposed to learn the language and culture, and so in order to have time to do this in the day, we needed someone to help us with household jobs. A young woman introduced herself, looking down on the floor and barely speaking. When I asked her if she would come back the next day, all I heard from her was a click. I repeated my question and there was another click. I was at a loss and decided to wait and see what would happen the next day. She came!

A few months later, we had a visitor from Germany. One of our Ghanaian colleagues knocked on our door and upon seeing our visitor, she enthusiastically exclaimed "She's fat!" (thankfully, in the local language!). Of course, the real meaning of what she said translates to: "She is beautiful! She is well! Germany must be a good country to live in! She is wealthy."

More recently, I visited a Kurdish family who had recently come to Germany. Their eight-year-old daughter had already learnt some German and asked her mother to draw her a "princess house". Unsatisfied with the result, she then asked me to draw her one. So, I drew her a beautiful German castle. But that wasn't right either. Out of frustration, she drew a few sweeping lines in the air to make out the shape of a curved roof and exclaimed "See! It has to be like *that*!" Then I realised: her concept of a "princess house" had been shaped by the Orient; she had thought of an oriental palace.

What is communication? The word comes from Latin and derives from 'communis', which means 'collective' or 'shared'. Communication aims to create 'common ground'. The success of any communication can be jeopardised if one or both parties prematurely assume, that one understands the other before this 'common ground' has actually been established. As shown by the example of the 'princess house', we each can interpret the same concept in different ways because of our own experiences. Communication should help to convey the very image that is in the mind of the speaker to the mind of the listener. The other examples above make it clear that communication is not just based on words, but also on art and music, gestures, body language as well as sounds (*clicks*). Incidentally, the lack of eye contact from the young woman was not a sign of disrespect, but exactly the opposite: in Ghana, for example, you don't look an older person in the eye – out of respect.

How could the communication in these examples have been better? In the first instance, I was culturally illiterate. Though both of us could speak English, at the time I had no idea about non-verbal communication, which is very common in Ghana. After a few years I adopted quite a few of these non-verbal forms of communicating into my own repertoire. In the beginning, however, I could have used a "cultural translator". By the way, our language assistant[60] later became our *culture coach*, drawing our attention to faux pas and answering our questions. He also explained to us why "You are fat!" is actually a compliment there. (In the post-war period – after years of hunger – it was a privilege to be fat in Germany too.)

In the third example, I might have paused for a moment. I had assumed that the little girl and I had the same idea of a 'princess house' because she already spoke some German. If I had thought for a moment however, I would've realised that she couldn't have seen any German castles yet. In the end I got the point because I was corrected by the girl's non-verbal feedback.

Feedback

Through discussion and feedback, both speaker and listener can become closer until they reach the highest possible level of understanding of what the one means and what the other understands. Of course, our own individual experiences serve as an aid to interpreting that which we are told. For example, a young German – who was on kitchen duty in an international college – was asked to go to the cellar and get some potatoes, from which to make *jacket potatoes*. Since she didn't know what jacket potatoes were, it was explained to her by the English cook, that they were 'potatoes cooked with the skin still on'. 'Aha!' she thought, "as in, *Pellkartoffeln*!" And so, she went and brought

---

[60] Since there were no textbooks for learning Dagbani, we met with a local language assistant, with whom we worked on vocabulary and grammar.

back small, evenly sized potatoes with a waxy skin. Later on, when I was talking to the English cook, I was shown the potatoes and she complained that they were much too small. I asked her how she explained *jacket potatoes* to the young German woman and then pointed out that *'potatoes cooked with the skin still on'* evoked a very different image in the UK than they do in Germany. The former picture an oven-baked potato with a thick skin, which should be large enough to suffice for one person. Germans, on the other hand, picture something akin to new potatoes, which are much smaller, often boiled, and a few of which are eaten among other things, rather than being the base of the meal. This example shows how we can make the mistake of thinking that the same term has a universal meaning across cultural backgrounds. Feedback is therefore crucial for avoiding misunderstandings and in getting to know how others think through different concepts. It prevents the listener from forming an image in their mind that the speaker does not intend.

How can we give good feedback?

We can ask things like: "Can you describe that a little more precisely? What does that mean to you?" Or we can briefly summarise what we think we have heard or understood and ask if that matches what the other is trying to express. So, discussion and feedback can grow our understanding. Feedback is particularly important when it comes to intercultural communication. Because of our different backgrounds and experiences, 'common ground' cannot be assumed automatically. We first need to create that by communicating.

The Communication Square Model[61]

Researchers in communication have found that every message being conveyed has four sides, regardless of culture. There's the *factual information*, the *appeal* to the receiver, the *self-revealing* of the sender and the *relationship* between the two parties. Depending on your personality and character, you may communicate these four sides in a particular way. For example, the sentence "The coffee pot is empty", can be a factual statement. But as an appeal, it means to the listener to prepare more coffee.

A visitor in an Us-Culture may say "Thank you, I don't want any tea." This can also be seen as a factual statement – that no tea is desired. However, this could also be seen as politeness: the visitor really might want tea but is used to being asked three times before they say yes, or that they are served tea anyway. The guest doesn't want to give the impression of being a burden (relationship). His 'no' is simply to show his politeness (self-revealing).

---

[61]   Kumbier, Schulz von Thun 2013, 12–14.

If the host comes from a Me-Culture and doesn't have any prior intercultural experience, then it's very likely that he will not see that his guest is simply being polite, and so the latter will continue to be thirsty. The host will not ask any further because he respects his guest's opinion and doesn't want to seem to be pressing him on the matter.

In the following sections, some other aspects will be presented which may influence intercultural communication.

Direct and Indirect Communication

In order to improve his culture and language learning in Ghana, my husband asked a local farmer if he could accompany him to the field. The farmer agreed and they arranged a time and place to meet. When the day came, my husband waited a long time, but the farmer didn't show up.

In some languages, the word 'no' is generally avoided. Instead, one draws on a repertoire of paraphrases and non-verbal cues to express something negative. We quickly learnt from our language coach that saying 'no' was seen as offensive in Ghana; instead, we should say "*Bieyne*", which means "tomorrow". "Tomorrow never comes." In a hierarching culture, it is also impossible to say 'no' to someone who has a higher position than you. It's generally accepted that 'no' goes unsaid and that the listener picks it up by reading between the lines.

"Yes" can mean "No" – but the reverse can also be true, as we have seen from the example of our thirsty friend on the top of the page. A little girl who grew up in the Philippines has come with her parents to visit Germany. She's offered something sweet and a drink, but she declines. So, she doesn't get anything. Later she complains to her mother, who explains to her that in Germany, 'no' actually means 'no', rather than an expression of politeness. That is to say, that one doesn't want to seem intrusive by asking again and again.

> *A biblical perspective:*
>
> *The Bible holds truth and love together and in tension: "Grace, mercy, and peace will be with us, from God the Father and from Jesus Christ the Father's Son, in truth and love" (2 John 3) and "speaking the truth in love" (Ephesians 4:15)*

People who are used to indirect communication are often shocked when they see people say what they think, without even considering whether it might be offensive. For these people, the important thing to understand is that in the West, ideas and people are separate (e.g. two people can engage in a debate, have different opinions and still be good friends,) and that talking factually is supposed to save time by getting to the point straight away. This may be perceived as being hard or unkind because it seems so 'cold and clinical', but it's usually not intended to be unkind, because it's all about the matter at hand, rather than anything personal.

Those who are used to direct communication should be aware of the effect that factual speech has when they are communicating across cultures. In an inter-cultural context, particularly in Us-Cultures, two people cannot reach a mutual understanding until they have eaten together and got to know one another personally. Business people in the West are now more aware of this.

Logic and Thought Processes

In an international consultation, I led a discussion group in which there were participants from Nigeria, Madagascar, the USA and Germany. To begin with, I pointed out that we most likely had different ways of thinking, and thus communicating. I suggested that we should all therefore enter the conversation with a willingness to understand one another.

In the course of the conversation, it so happened that one of the Germans threw in a "but! ..." and argued for his point objectively, whereupon a Nigerian sought to create harmony because he feared that a dispute had broken out. He, in turn, wrapped his line of argument in stories, which appeared long-winded to the Westerners who were waiting for him to get to the point.

Different cultures 'think' differently. Each has its own distinct form of logic. A good example of this is the approach of two teachers from different backgrounds teaching the same subject.

A German *homiletics'* teacher (preaching lessons), would tell his students to consider the counterarguments of the audience. There is always a 'but' in German thinking. Their thought process is shaped **dialectically**, and for them it is simply a matter of intellectual honesty. For an American teacher, it would never occur to them to factor in counterarguments. Why over-complicate everything? He would guide his students to argue linearly (first, second, third, etc.) and then to draw a conclusion. When this form of argument is put to Germans, they sometimes feel like they're being 'sold something'.

In Asian religions and partly in folk-religious worldviews, life is under the influence of the cyclical doctrine of reincarnation. This informs the logical process, which runs like a spiral. One could say that this kind of argument is *intuitive* and associative, so that one gradually comes to higher levels of knowledge. *Existential* thinking is similar to this. It seeks to rouse the emotions and to convey ideas via experience. Facts alone are not convincing; you intuitively reach out for a new truth that you cannot yet grasp.[62] This corresponds to the postmodern way of thinking, and it is also found especially in Finland and Russia.

Most cultures think contextually, rather than abstractly. For them, it is difficult to isolate the most important point. They think in terms of stories, proverbs and pictures, and so they communicate accordingly. Examples and stories help to create mental categories; they also help in addressing grievances without anyone having to be directly confronted.

What happens if you don't adapt to the logic of the others? Telling long stories to those looking for a defined point, will be just as misunderstood as talking about concepts for which there is no corresponding word in another language.

An Example from Ethiopia[63]

A teacher reprimanded two students who came an hour late for classes. On the last day of the course, one of them stood up to ask a question. He told the story of a horse, who worked hard and then would come to the waterhole to drink. However, someone had stirred the mud under the water so much, that the horse couldn't drink at all. The student finally asked: "What should be done to solve this problem?"

What's this about? Publicly reprimanding the students' lateness caused them shame. This kept them from concentrating on the events of the lesson, which they were previously looking forward to. In order to restore their honour and overcome their shame, the student chose to express his grievance through a story instead and not to directly criticize his teacher.

---

[62]   Roembke 2000, 163–164, nach Lehtinen.
[63]   Hesselgrave 1991, 326.

Communication Behaviours

A model by Richard Lewis explains different communication behaviour.[64] Lewis assumes three different modes of behaviour, which he calls linear-active, multi-active and reactive. In addition to the pure forms, there are also mixed forms.

The **linear-active** behaviour characterizes the typical Western businessman (this is a stereotype, however) who stays "cool", restricts himself to the facts and plans decisively. He communicates directly by the most convenient means, often preferring to write emails or make phone calls. He is more task- than people-orientated, and generally adheres to rules and laws. According to Mary Douglas (see p. 31), he represents the institutionalizing culture.

Cultures that are relationship and family-oriented (Latin America, the Mediterranean region, the Arab world, Africa) are **multi-active**. People in this culture talk a lot and use a lot of hand gestures. They are warm, impulsive, emotional, and frequently engage in physical touch (though not necessarily people of the opposite sex; instead, two men can be seen walking hand in hand, simply as platonic friends). You talk and listen at the same time; silence is perceived as uncomfortable. Communication should take place in person if possible, not via email or telephone. People like to look for creative solutions and "shortcuts", use contacts and see rules more as suggestions than as norms. Despite the widespread ability to read and write, people prefer to communicate orally.

A Brazilian once told me that upon starting a job in England, she was presented with a handbook so that she could familiarise herself with her new responsibilities. She said that this had been useless to her. She expected a personal briefing.

In the aforementioned film *'My Big Fat Greek Wedding'*, conflict arises between the two families because of their different communication behaviours. Whereas the Greek family communicates with great warmth, loudness and closeness, the American family is cool, reserved, and they find themselves overwhelmed by it all.

In **reactive** cultures (especially in Eastern Asia, but also Finland to a certain extent) people are reserved, polite and respectful, very good listeners and willing to compromise. Silence in a conversation is a sign of respect and it is needed for one to formulate their own opinion on a particular matter. Questions help to better understand the position of the other, as well as to avoid misunderstandings. Harmony and consensus are the goal; confrontation is

---

[64] Cross-Culture. *The Lewis Model*. http://www.crossculture.com/about-us/the-model.

avoided as much as possible. Since communication is often done with just a few words, atmosphere and non-verbal communication play an important role. The Japanese speak of "reading the air".

Non-verbal Communication

Through an African woman who was granted asylum in Germany, I became aware of how quickly non-verbal communication can be misunderstood. Many gestures that we Germans are used to, such as raising our head to greet someone when both hands are full, were interpreted by her as rejection or aggression. Gestures have different meanings, depending on the cultural reference. In the Philippines it was enough to simply raise your eyebrows when greeting someone. In many countries it is taboo to use the left hand for eating, greeting or giving gifts because it is used for cleaning after using the toilet. Eye contact is also subject to special rules, as there are social differences based on age and gender. Children avoid eye contact with the elderly, and women do so with men. Showing the soles of your feet communicates disrespect.

Important objects are given honour by placing them in the highest point in the room. Pictures often hang right under the ceiling; religious books are kept on the top shelf and are never placed on the floor. Clothing speaks as well. It's not just in the West that the saying is true: "the clothes make the man". In cultures where the external is still important, there is the notion of 'Sunday Best': shoes are well-shined, there is not a hair out of place and women make use of makeup and jewellery. Many Me-Cultures no longer hold these things in such high regard. Before going to the Philippines on a trip, it was a useful tip for me to bring a nice dress, decent shoes and lipstick. I had mistakenly thought "A poor land with poor people – simple clothing would be appropriate."

Colours also have their own particular meanings. When going to a funeral, for example, the Ashanti people in Ghana would wear brown, red and black coloured fabrics. In India, one would wear white instead, and in Thailand it would be black and white.

Verbal Communication

Language is an essential part of communication. That's why it's so important to learn foreign languages: to be able to communicate with others. It is, however, understandable that some errors and misunderstandings will occur.

A young American is trying to woo a Chinese woman with a particularly beautiful gift. She says that she thinks it's "arrogant". The young man is shocked and immediately asks for forgiveness, which the young woman is confused by. It then occurs to him that there is not much distinction in pronounciation between 'L' and 'R'. In fact, she thought the gift was *"elegant"*, but she had accidentally pronounced the word as "arrogant".[65]

A language not only allows us to express ourselves, but we can also learn a lot about other cultures, their way of thinking and about the categories in which they think. Language brings order to our thinking. If you take a list of different terms, e.g. groups of people, animals and plants, and have them summarized by different people in categories, you learn something about how these people perceive the world. In this way, Gailyn van Rheenen found out that in Haiti trees and women were grouped together as *"fruit-bearing"*, while in a certain part of East Africa women and cows were classified as *"things that are ruled over, which can be exchanged as bride-prices"*.[66]

When there are many words for an object that show subtle differences in meaning, one can be certain that this takes up a lot of space in people's thoughts and lives. For example, the Inuit in Greenland have numerous expressions for the nature of snow and the Dagombas in Northern Ghana for the different types of hoes used in field work.

Despite a common language, misunderstandings arise when there are different concepts surrounding the same terms. An "Anglo-EU Translation Guide" can be found on the Internet, which shows in a funny way how the literal meaning of something said can express the opposite of what is meant. "You must come for dinner" is just a polite phrase for the British and Americans that is not meant to be serious, but if you pay attention to the exact wording, then it can evoke the expectation of an invitation. My husband and I have experienced misunderstandings in our intercultural work when a 'recommendation' was made by the supervisor. We considered it as a team, but then rejected it, only for it to be stated later on, that this 'recommendation' was not up for debate, and that it was in fact an 'instruction from above'.

Ethno-Music

Music does not communicate internationally! I understood this in a seminar about ethnomusicology. We learnt to sing a South American song with a harmony. For me it sounded like a dirge with lots of dissonance. However, we eventually learnt that it was a song of joy!

There is such a thing as "heart music". In many churches and Christian communities there is tension between the generations because of the musical style

---

[65]   Heilsarmee 2011, 5.

[66]   van Rheenen 1991, 47–48.

of the songs that are sung during worship time. Each generation has their own heart music which goes back to the time of their own youth.

Development aid agencies use heart music for instance to teach the basic rules of hygiene by putting instructional texts to native tunes which the learners love to sing. Through this the content of the lessons sinks in deeply.

Summary

- Communication aims at creating 'common ground' between what the sender (speaker) means and what the receiver (hearer) understands.

- Feedback is a good tool to ensure that 'common ground' is created.

- The communication square model can be a help in analysing what happens in a given communicative situation.

- Intercultural communication means taking account of cultural peculiarities as there are direct and indirect communication, varying logic and thought processes, cultural behaviour in communicative situations, the importance and meaning of non-verbal communication, ethno-music, etc.

- Language is an indispensable means of communication. Learning a foreign language is a perfect vehicle for learning the culture and way of thinking of the people who speak this language.

Chapter 12

With the following scenarios you can test your intercultural communication skills.

Chinese Whispers

An African student in Europe is unhappy about the way the group meetings she regularly attends are conducted. She talks to a member of the leadership team who passes the message on. The leader of the group re-structures the meetings according to the wishes of the student – at least according to what he thinks her wish is. At the end of the school year he learns from other people that he is accused of not having reacted to the earlier criticism.

Do you perceive the pitfalls in communication in this example? What could have been done differently and better?

First of all, in a European context it is not helpful to communicate through a mediator – though this was probably the default way for the African student. There was no possibility to directly clarify matters through questions. The student *assumes* that her message had been understood which obviously was not the case. Then, the responsibility would have been with the leader to invite an open *feedback* and to let the group discuss how the group meetings could be designed. He *assumes* that he (himself) had found a solution without involving *feedback* from the student(s).

Back and Forth

A Brazilian and a Korean are in a room and chat. The following pattern repeats itself: He moves a step forward – she goes a step back. When they end their talk, they find themselves in the opposite corner of the room.

Can you explain why these two kept moving while talking?

The Brazilian is from a multi-active cultural background; closeness and touch are normal and important. He feels at ease when he is relatively close to the person he talks to. The Korean comes from a reactive culture in which people are more reserved and keep a certain distance. Whenever he takes a step towards her to feel at ease, she steps back to remain in her own comfort zone.

Work on a Public Holiday

Mr Miller runs a conference centre.

Mr Ali Hamid is relatively new to this country and has recently learned the language. He currently helps Mr Miller as an intern.

On one occasion Mr Miller asks him: "I wondered if you were free to help me set up everything for the next conference. I know it's a holiday but I really need help."

To which Mr Hamid replies: "I understand."

"So, will you come?"

"Yes."

"Great." This seems to be settled.

As an afterthought Mr Hamid says: "Actually, that day is an important day."

"In what way?" asks Mr Miller.

"It's my father's birthday," replies Mr Hamid.

"Well, that's great! I hope you will have a great time together!"

To which Mr Hamid responds: "Thank you very much!"

Will Mr Hamid come to work on that public holiday?

It is very likely that Mr Miller will be waiting for his intern on that public holiday in vain. Why? Mr Hamid first tries to avoid saying "yes or no", but when asked directly modifies his 'Yes' by contrasting Mr Miller's plans with his own. Mr Miller probably only hears the 'Yes' and understands everything else that is said through this seeming affirmation. Mr Hamid cannot say 'No' to his boss because according to his cultural background, it would be insulting to do so. So, he tries to communicate indirectly. For Mr Miller it seems to be clear that work first and family later can be combined. Not so for Mr Hamid. We can assume that he comes from an Us-Culture in which a family get-together is of utmost priority.

The "Chill" Weekend

A newly wed couple finally had a free weekend together. *Chill* – that's what it should be – they have agreed upon that. She cooks a good meal, afterwards he goes off for a nap while she does the dishes. When she has finished she puts on her walking boots and tells him that they can now go for a walk. "I thought we were going to have a *chill* weekend", is his appalled reaction.

In what ways could a clarifying talk before the weekend have been helpful for these newly-weds?

Quite obviously both have very different ideas what "chill" means, depending on how this was defined in their childhood families. Had they chatted about *chill* weekends in their childhood they would have realised the differences.

Instead of basing the whole weekend on assumptions they could have agreed on how they wanted to spend the weekend together. Communication could have helped to reach more 'common-ness' (or common ground)[67] in their understanding.

Decision Making in an Intercultural Team

New leaders were to be elected, not just by a majority vote, but with as much consensus as possible. In order to reach this consensus, it was important to talk with and listen to one another. Those team members from a Western cultural background were actively debating. Then the person facilitating this discussion (who was not part of the team) pushed for a decision. However, one team member noticed that the colleagues from Asia had not voiced their opinion. Their body language gave away that they were not happy with the direction the discussion had taken. Only after having been explicitly invited they shared their opinion.

Try to explain the behaviour of the different groups of team members in this culturally mixed team.

In a democratic system people are raised to voice their opinion openly. That is why the Western colleagues engage in the discussion. In hierarching and maybe reactive cultures, team members are also asked what they think but this normally happens individually when eating together or between meetings. It is the task of the moderator to elicit the thoughts of the various people beforehand and to then mention them in the discussion so that everyone feels represented and heard. In the above-mentioned situation, there had obviously been no previous talks with the Asian colleagues. Due to their cultural expectations it was difficult for them to express themselves in a wider circle, especially with the opinion being in contrast to what the majority thought. All the more important it was to read their non-verbal clues and to invite them directly to express their thoughts.

A Question of Competence?[68]

A Japanese multinational company sends one of their most competent workers to Germany into a nearly all German team. After a year of working there he still asks questions like: "Would you agree to involve Mr X?" or "Does this

---

[67]   This is an intended play of words: commun-ication creates common-ness.

[68]   Rez et al. 2006, 54–57.

match your ideas?" The German boss by then lets slip that he doubts the competence of this co-worker. The Japanese man then asks to be transferred back to Japan.

In this situation the communication square could be used to explain the misunderstanding (see page 65)

The Japanese co-worker asks for factual information which his German colleagues interpret as evidence of his incompetence (self-revealing) and as calls for help (appeal). However, this is not the intention of the questions. The Japanese co-worker uses them to establish relationship. He communicates from his side: "I enjoy working together with you. I respect your position." This implicit message of relationship and appreciation is lost on the German colleagues.

Too late

In Ghana we employed a lovely widow as our domestic help. Our agreement was for her to work from eight to twelve. However, often she started later, especially in the early days. As a very punctual German I found that difficult because I wanted to plan my mornings. Communication was difficult: I was not yet able to speak her mother tongue nor was she able to speak English, so we had to communicate via our language helper (a person who helped us learn the local language for lack of books and language courses). After some time, she became more punctual. However, I too, had to learn some things about the local conditions.

Try to find possible reasons for her delays in the mornings.

I could have simply said: "*African time* – in Africa being late is normal." This is a stereotype, but there is also some truth in it because in Africa time is not understood as a *point* in time, but as a time *span*. There were, however, more reasons for the late arrivals of our househelper. What I had not considered at all was the fact that she did not have a watch, nor was she able to read the time. We gave her a watch with hands, and after work we practised reading it. Furthermore, I discovered that there were people who came to visit her just at the time when she was due to go to work. By and by the neighbours understood that this was an inconvenient time for visits. On rainy days we waited for our domestic help in vain, for getting wet always carried the danger of contracting pneumonia. In case of a death in the family she did not come to work for two weeks. We were then informed by a messenger. Later, after she had moved and had to use public transport, her arrival was even more irregular as the car or bus would only leave when it was full. Expecting punctuality then would not have made any sense.

A Procedure for Granting the Right of Asylum[69]

Ibrahim is informed that his application had been turned down. His German friend scans the letter together with him to understand the reason for this rejection. They accuse Ibrahim of being "not credible". The two friends read again the minutes of the first interview. They discover that some facts were not represented correctly in those minutes, and that the rejection of his application is based on those misrepresented facts. Ibrahim had waived his right to get the minutes re-translated into his mother tongue so that he had not discovered the mistake. His German friend knows his story and therefore finds the fault now.

You may want to reflect about the causes for severe misunderstandings in the procedure for granting the right of asylum.

Putting ourselves into the situation of such an interview may act as an eye-opener: Ibrahim as the applicant has a history, a story that he wants to share. Some of those things are difficult to understand in a German context because of the great cultural differences as he well knows.

The moderator's task is to listen to the story of the applicant and to check at the same time whether it is genuine, not exaggerated nor simply learned by heart. Therefore, he wants to know many personal details. Should the applicant begin to tell the story in too much detail (for instance, to explain cultural issues) then this may appear like an evasive manoeuvre. The moderator can only fall back on his own pool of experiences.

The translator is probably most able to relate to the applicant, on the basis of culture and from his life experience. He is a potential culture broker. However, if he originates from a people or religious group other than the applicants, then this may have an effect on his attitude towards the group the applicant belongs to, which in turn could influence the translation.

The moderator not only listens, but also steers the interview. He can interrupt the report at any time in order to ask clarifying questions. The applicant, by contrast, has neither the right – nor probably the courage – to clarify facts when (or if) he thinks that he was misunderstood.

The moderator "filters" what he hears – whether consciously or subconsciously – in various ways: What facts have I heard? What – in my opinion – is the meaning of what was said? How can I make sense from what I heard? How should I assess it?

---

[69]   Following Rienzner 2011. Please note that this paragraph is based on observations made in Austria. The communication process may be different in other places.

All of this taken together results in the interpretation of the applicant's story which finally needs to be put into the formal language of minutes and reports. And for this final text the applicant is held responsible.[70]

---

[70] Rienzner 2011, 79.

Afterword

"You Europeans are all so ... " We had a new colleague from Asia in our team who was in the process of getting used to living in a strange culture. In order to be able to cope with all the cultural differences, she used stereotypes and generalisations. My inner reaction was: "You don't know me. Why are you judging me?"

By reading this book you have gained a basic knowledge of cultural difference. You may now be tempted to put others into a 'box' and by doing so, use stereotypes. Every person has been shaped by a cultural background, but first and foremost they are individuals with their own personality – and this is how they want to be perceived. In addition to this, the reality of life of your friends from other cultures is much more complex than this little booklet could ever depict.

It is very likely that in intercultural encounters, certain things will be a mystery to you – and you may even get exasperated about them. In such cases it may be a good exercise to reflect on what these reactions tell you about yourself and your own cultural orientation. After all, self-awareness is the first step towards understanding others better.

Therefore: keep what you learnt in this book at the back of your mind and get involved with people from other cultures. Share about your family and ask about theirs. Who does what? When? What is important? ... This is how you can get to know and understand each other better. And I hope that you will experience how the cultural theory you learnt in this book will become more vivid and coherent as your own 'collection' of intercultural experiences grows.

Appendix

Many Christians who read the Bible and want to live accordingly to it may wonder: What is a biblical culture? Or: Is there a particular culture that corresponds with the Bible?

In order to answer this question, we need to keep in mind the following facts:

1. Culture is God ordained. God gave man the "cultural mandate" (Genesis 1:28,[71] 2:15[72]).

2. Each culture has structures and values which are not in accordance with God's will but sinful (Romans 11:32,[73] Galatians 3:22a[74]). We are captives of our own cultures.[75]

3. The Bible tells us how God acted in history through the lives of ordinary people who lived at a certain point in time at a specific place with their specific cultural orientation.

4. Therefore, we find different cultures in the Bible. Abraham, Isaac and Jacob (Genesis 12–50) lived as nomads with their extended families. Even though the patriarch was the head of the family the women had a say, too. Social roles seemed to have been flexible so that it was okay for Jacob to help in the house while his brother Esau went hunting. The twin brothers were in competition about the right of the first born. When Esau married, he chose a wife from a different tribe without consulting with his parents. Jacob and his uncle Laban later negotiated the wages for seven years of service – instead of the older man simply fixing it. All these are the elements of an *individuating culture,*[76] as exemplified earlier by the Deni-Indians of the Brazilian rain forest. (p. 38).

The patriarchal family clan developed over time into a hierarchic tribal structure and finally into a people under a common leader. These were Moses and Joshua to begin with, then different judges and kings. At the time of the New Testament the Jewish family culture was *hierarchical.* It was the men who

---

[71] And God blessed them. And God said to them, "Be fruitful and multiply and fill the earth and subdue it, and have dominion over the fish of the sea and over the birds of the heavens and over every living thing that moves on the earth."

[72] The Lord God took the man and put him in the Garden of Eden to work it and keep it.

[73] For God has consigned all to disobedience, that he may have mercy on all

[74] But the Scripture imprisoned everything under sin …

[75] Lingenfelter 1998, 21.

[76] Lingenfelter 1998, 107–109.

made decisions and fulfilled their social and religious duties. In this they were supported by the family clan. Marriages were arranged. The Mosaic Law gave structure to their lives. Children were expected to obey their parents and to submit and thus to honour them. This is exemplified by the stories of Zachariah and Elizabeth and Mary and Joseph (Luke 1–2).[77] These hierarchical structures can still be found today in the Near and Middle East.

5. Next to the Jewish culture the Bible gives us a glimpse into other cultures, for example the Egyptian at the time of the Pharaohs (Exodus 1–9) or the Babylonian (Nehemiah 1 and Daniel 1–5) as well as the Roman and the Greek through reports in the Acts of the Apostles and especially through house and church tables[78] in the epistles (Ephesians 5:22–6,9; Colossians 3:18–4:1; 1 Peter 2:18–3:7).

6. The question remains whether there is a culture that is binding for all Christians. Sherwood Lingenfelter denies this.[79] No matter whether we wonder who should have the authority in the family or what should a good leader look like, Christians are not bound to copy *one* cultural model but essentially to become more like Jesus in our character and the way we relate to one another.[80] The Bible[81] values diversity that comes together in unity (1 Corinthians 12, Ephesians 4:3,11–13). Mutual submission (Ephesians 5:21)[82] and love (Romans 12:9),[83] keeping the peace (Romans 12:18),[84] forgiveness (Colossians 3:13),[85] speaking good about and to one another (Romans 12:14),[86] these are important pillars in a Christian community that is marked by the presence of the Holy Spirit. Identity is no longer first and

---

[77] Lingenfelter 1998, 109–112.

[78] The term 'Haustafel' (home structure) goes back to Martin Luther. They portray Christian social systems in the New Testament that explain how relationships in the Christian family and church were to be lived out. These kind of writings were common in the Hellenistic-Roman world of that time. More information can be found with Bernhard Mutschler (see bibliography).

[79] Lingenfelter 1998, 113+116.

[80] Ibid,113, 117.

[81] The following points are taken from Lingenfelter's concept of 'Covenant Community' (2008, 76).

[82] … submitting to one another out of reverence for Christ.

[83] Let love be genuine. Abhor what is evil; hold fast to what is good.

[84] If possible, so far as it depends on you, live peaceably with all.

[85] … bearing with one another and, if one has a complaint against another, forgiving each other; as the Lord has forgiven you, so you also must forgive.

[86] Bless those who persecute you; bless and do not curse them.

foremost defined by one's cultural origin but by belonging to the chosen people of God (1 Peter 2:9).[87]

7. Mary Douglas and Sheryl Silzer[88] emphasize that the strengths of one cultural type are the weaknesses of another. The *individuating* cultural type gives freedom to the individual to trust in God in their decision making instead of in human rules (*institutionalizing*), tradition (*hierarching*), or in group consensus (*interrelating*). However, they need Us-Cultures to understand how their individualistic decisions affect others. From the institutionalizing and hierarching cultural types they can learn how to be more structured.

   Someone growing up in an *institutionalizing* culture is used to order and has learnt to follow rules. This can be a help when it comes to following God's rules. A Christian with such a cultural imprint needs the support of people from the individuating cultural type to discern abuse of power, and from hierarching and interrelating backgrounds to learn to see other people with their needs.

   Loyalty towards the community, respect towards leaders, and care for one another – these are the strengths of the *hierarching* type. However, they need correction from individuating and interrelating cultural types to discern potential abuse of power which could come about through the leader or the community (for instance through social pressure to achieve conforming behaviour) or through forming of cliques (and the resulting ostracising of others).

   Interrelating people are examples in sharing of resources and in caring for one another. They can be in danger to bow to social pressure in their decisions rather than follow biblical principles. To detect these cultural pitfalls, they need help from those from Me-Cultures.

   The Bible encourages us to be transformed into the image of Jesus.[89] This can happen particularly in those settings where people from different cultures interact with one another in a teachable and humble way.

8. When reading the Bible we have the tendency to read it with our own 'cultural glasses'. Read the following verse and ask yourself who is addressed: "If we confess our sins, he is faithful and just to forgive us our sins and to cleanse us from all unrighteousness." (1 John 1:9) People from Me-Cultures have the tendency to relate the verse to themselves as individuals. 'We' becomes 'I' in their minds. As a matter of fact, the verse says 'we', and so

---

[87] But you are a chosen race, a royal priesthood, a holy nation, a people for his own possession…

[88] Silzer 2011, 148–149.

[89] 2 Corinthians 3:18.

people from Us-Cultures will understand a communal confession of sins as biblical and appropriate.

Many stories in the Bible have a strong honour/shame dynamic which people from a justice-guilt orientation may not catch in most cases. In a German class, I once narrated the story of the persistent widow (Luke 18:1–7) to a group of migrant ladies. In verses 4–5 the reason is mentioned why the judge finally gives in to her: "Though I neither fear God nor respect man, yet because this widow keeps bothering me, I will give her justice, so that she will not beat me down by her continual coming." Literally, it says: 'come and hit me in the face'.

I thought for a long time that the judge was so fed up with the woman that he finally gave in to her. But when reading carefully – and not all translations make that clear – one understands that the real reason for the judge to change his approach to her was his fear of being ridiculed by the widow through a blow into his face. The migrant ladies understood that immediately and and enjoyed the story immensely.[90]

---

[90] Books from the following authors can help to understand the Bible in its cultural background: Richards, E. Randolph und Brandon J. O'Brien, 2012; Bailey, Kenneth E., 2008; Georges, Jayson und Mark D. Baker, 2016.

Acknowledgments

Originally, I wanted to jot down some things about culture for our son who thought about studying ethnology. But when I read parts of my script to a group of hobby writers at a writing workshop, they encouraged me to work towards publication. Thank you!

My colleague Ilse-Marie Neuroth outdid herself in proof-reading my German drafts, making suggestions, challenging me to write in an easy-to-understand style. Thanks so much!

I am grateful to the team of the ESCT in Korntal that took interest in the book and facilitated the German publication. Thank you!

Many thanks to my husband and son who encouraged me not to give up and to keep going.

For the English publication I very much thank Rev Currie for his kind foreword. Joseph Barnes did a marvellous job in translating a German book not only into the English language, but also into its culture. Thanks, too, to Marion Barnes for proof-reading and a long-standing friendship!

Bibliography

Andersson, Per J. 2016. *Vom Inder, der mit dem Fahrrad bis nach Schweden fuhr, um dort seine große Liebe wiederzufinden. Eine wahre Geschichte.* Köln: Bastei Lübbe.

Andrews, Colin E. 2015a. *Five Rude Things Honor-Shame Cultures say.* http://honorshame.com/5-rude-actually-polite-things-honor-shame-cultures-say (02.09.2015)

Andrews, Colin E. 2015b. *Five Shameful Things Westerners say.* http://honorshame.com/5-shameful-things-westerners-say/ (15.02.2017)

Bailey, Kenneth E. 2008. *Jesus Through Middle Eastern Eyes: Cultural Studies in the Gospels.* London: SPCK.

Blick. 2016. Messi verärgert Ägypter mit Schuhgeschenk. http://www.blick.ch/sport/fussball/international/messi-veraergert-aegypter-mit-schuh-geschenk-wir-wurden-in-7000-jahren-nie-so-beleidigt-id4864017.html (31.01.2017)

DiGennaro, Debbi. 2017. *Acclimated to Africa: Cultural Competence for Westerners.* Dallas: SIL.

Earley, P.C. and Ang, S. 2003. *Cultural Intelligence: Individual Interactions Across Cultures.* Stanford: Stanford Business Books.

Elmer, Duane. 2006. *Cross-Cultural Servanthood: Serving the World in Christlike Humility.* Downers Grove: IVP.

Gardner, E. Howard, Mihaly Csikszentmihalyi, William Damon. 2002. *Good Work: When Excellence and Ethics Meet.* New York: Basic Books.

Georges, Jayson. 2016a. *The 3D Gospel: Ministry in Guilt, Shame, and Fear Cultures.* 2nd ed. N.d.: Time Press.

Georges, Jayson. 2016b. *To be or not to be ... a Patron.* http://honorshame.com/to-be-or-not-to-be-a-patron/ (15. 02. 2017)

Georges, Jayson 2017a. *Guilt-Innocence Cultures are WEIRD.* http://honorshame.com/guilt-innocence-cultures-weird/ (aufgerufen 15.2.2017)

Georges, Jayson. 2017b. *The Culture Test.* http://theculturetest.com/survey

Georges, Jayson and Mark D. Baker. 2016. *Ministering in Honor-Shame Cultures: Biblical Foundations and Practical Essentials.* Downers Grove: IVP.

Hall, Edward, T. 1976. *Beyond Culture.* Np.: Anchor Books.

Hanisch, Horst. 2016. *Welcome to Germany Knigge: Umgangsformen, Verhaltensmuster, gesellschaftliches Miteinander im deutschsprachigen Europa.* Norderstedt: Books on Demand.

Heilsarmee. 2011. Gesichter der Heilsarmee. *Heilsarmee Magazin* 25/11, 4–5.

Henrich, J., Heine, S. J., & Norenzayan, A. 2010. The Weirdest People in the World?. *Behavioral and Brain Sciences, 33* (2–3), 61–83.

Hesselgrave, David J. 1991. *Communicating Christ Cross-Culturally: An Introduction to Missionary Communication.* 2nd ed. Grand Rapids: Zondervan.

Hofstede, Geert. N.d. *National Culture.* https://geert-hofstede.com/national-culture.html

Hofstede, Geert and Gert Jan Hofstede. 2005. *Culture and Organizations: Software of the Mind.* 2nd ed. New York: McGraw-Hill.

Jahn, Egbert. 2014. Sprachliche Assimilation aller Staatsangehörigen oder Minderheitenschutz: der Präzedenzfall Åland-Inseln. *Frankfurter Montags-Vorlesungen: Politische Streitfragen in zeitgeschichtlicher Perspektive* (Neue Folge 30). http://fkks.uni-mannheim.de/montagsvorlesung/aland/zsframov30_net_aland_49.pdf (22.08.2017)

Käser, Lothar. 2001. *Angewandte Anthropologie in Deutschland aus der Sicht von Afrikanern und Asiaten. Em* 17(3): 91–94.

Käser, Lothar. 2014a. *Foreign Cultures: An Introduction to Ethnology.* Nürnberg: VTR.

Käser, Lothar. 2014b. *Animism: A Cognitive Approach. An Introduction to the Basic Notions.* Nürnberg: VTR.

Kumbier, Dagmar und Friedemann Schulz von Thun (Hg.). 2006. *Interkulturelle Kommunikation: Methoden, Modelle, Beispiele.* Reinbek: Rowohlt.

Kwast, Lloyd. 1981. Understanding Culture. In *Perspectives on the World Christian Movement,* Hg. Ralph Winter und Stephen C. Hawthorne, 361–364. Pasadena: William Carey.

Lanier, Sarah A. 2000. *Foreign to Familiar: A Guide to Understanding Hot- and Cold-Climate Cultures.* Hagerstown: McDougal.

Lehtinen, Kalevi. N.d. "Through the Prism." Unpublished.

Lidorio, Ronaldo. 2007. *Von Furcht befreit: Die Entstehung der Kirche unter den Konkomba.* Linz: OM Books.

Lidorio, Ronaldo. 2007. *Unafraid of the Sacred Forest: The Birth of a Church in an African Tribe.* Gerrards Cross: WEC International.

Lingenfelter, Sherwood. 1998. *Transforming Culture: A Challenge for Christian Mission.* Grand Rapids: Baker Books.

Lingenfelter, Sherwood G. 2008. *Leading Cross-Culturally: Covenant Relationships for Effective Christian Leadership.* Grand Rapids: Baker.

Livermore, David A. 2009. *Leading with Cultural Intelligence.* New York: AMACOM.

Lübbehausen, Hanne. 2014. *Japaner fahren ihre Gebrauchten zum Seelenreiniger.* http://www.welt.de/motor/article130054610/Japaner-fahren-ihre-Gebrauchten-zum-Seelenreiniger.html (17.1.2017)

Luzbetak, Louis J. 1963. *The Church and Cultures.* Techny: Divine Word.

Malinowski, Bronislaw. 1975. *Eine wissenschaftliche Theorie der Kultur. Und andere Aufsätze.* Suhrkamp taschenbuch der wissenschaft 104. Frankfurt am Main: Suhrkamp.

Map-Consult. N.d. *Das Hofstede Kulturmodell.* http://www.map-consult.com/de/culture-diversity/das-hofstede-kulturmodell.

Meyer, Erin. 2015. *The Culture Map: Decoding How People Think, Lead, And Get Things Done Across Cultures.* New York: Public Affairs.

Mühlan, Eberhard. 2016. *Cross-Cultural Couples: Loving against all odds.* Braunschweig: MuehlanMedien.

Müller, Roland. 2010. *The Messenger, the Message, the Community: Three Critical Issues for the Cross-Cultural Church-Planter.* Canbooks.

Mutschler, Bernhard. 2013. Haustafel. *Bibelwissenschaft.de* https://www.bibelwissenschaft.de/stichwort/46870/ (4.8.2017)

Oehrlein, Josef. 2012. Falklandkrieg: Ein Abenteuer mit verheerenden Folgen. *FAZ* http://www.faz.net/aktuell/politik/ausland/falkland-krieg-ein-abenteuer-mit-verheerenden-folgen-11701990.html (22.08.2017)

Pollock, David C. and Ruth E van Reken. 2009. *Third Culture Kids: Growing Up Among Worlds.* London: Nicholas Brealey.

Qureshi, Nabeel. 2014. *Seeking Allah, Finding Jesus: A Devout Muslim Encounters Christianity.* Grand Rapids: Zondervan.

Rez, Helmut, Kraemer, Monika und Reiko Kobayashi-Weinsziehr. 2006. Warum Karl und Keizo sich nerven: Eine Reise zum systematischen Verständnis interkultureller Missverständnisse. In *Interkulturelle Kommunikation: Methoden, Modelle, Beispiele*, Hg. Dagmar Kumbier und Friedemann Schulz von Thun, 28–72. Reinbek: Rowohlt.

Rich. 2016. *Five Lessons I Learned From Being a Terrible Patron.* http://honorshame.com/terrible-patron-5-lessons/ (15.02.2017)

Richards, E. Randolph and Brandon J. O'Brien. 2012. *Misreading Scripture with Western Eyes: Removing Cultural Blinders to Better Understand the Bible.* Downers Grove: IVP.

Rienzner, Martina. 2011. *Interkulturelle Kommunikation in Asylverfahren.* Frankfurt/Main: Peter Lang.

Roembke, Lianne. 2000. *Building Credible Multicultural Teams.* Pasadena: William Carey.

Rose, Dave. 2017. Erfahrungen mit einer schamorientierten Kultur. *Allianzmission aktuell,* Februar/März 2017, 5.

Silzer, Sheryl Takagi. 2014. *Biblical Multicultural Teams: Applying Biblical Truth to Cultural Differences.* Pasadena: William Carey International University Press.

Storti, Craig. 1998. *Figuring Foreigners out: A Practical Guide.* Yarmouth: Intercultural Press.

Telelangue. 2011. *Geert Hofstede und die Kulturdimensionen-Theorie – Übersicht,* http://news.telelangue.com/de/2011/09/kulturdimensionen.

Trompenaars, Fons and Charles Hampden-Turner. 1998. *Riding the Waves of Culture: Understanding Diversity in Global Business.* 2nd ed. New York: McGraw Hill.

van Rheenen, Gailyn. 1991. *Communicating Christ in Animistic Contexts.* Grand Rapids: Baker.

Winter, Ralph D. und Steven C. Hawthorne (Hgs.). 1981. *Perspectives on the World Christian Movement: A Reader.* Pasadena: William Carey.

Glossary

Culture: 'Culture is a design for living. It is a plan according to which society adapts itself to its physical, social, and ideational environment… Cultures are but different answers to essentially the same human problems.' (Luzbetak 1963, 60–61, cited in Hesselgrave 1991, 100)

Culture-based Judging System (CbJS): is the way people decide what is right or wrong based on their cultural upbringing. Strong emotions may accompany these judgments, often reflecting the way our parents re-enforced their cultural values when bringing their children up. The CbJS gives away which cultural type we belong to. The term was coined by Sheryl Silzer (2014)

Communication Square: it goes back to communication theorist Schulz von Thun and says that every message can be heard in four different ways – the *factual information*, the *appeal* to the receiver, the *self-revealing* of the sender and as a message about the *relationship* between the two parties

Corruption: in the strictest sense, the word means 'rotten' or 'rancid'. In the context of Us-Cultures, it's considered corrupt when one doesn't give advantages to a member of their group, even though that person could. In the context of Me-Cultures, the opposite is true: it's considered corrupt when one doesn't uphold "equality for all" and it is seen as unfair if one shows favouritism

Ethnicity: describes a positive cultural understanding of oneself that has no intention of raising itself above people with other cultural identities

Ethnocentrism: is the attitude and belief that our cultural way of doing things and judging others are the only correct way; **racism** would be a very strong form of ethnocentrism

Ethnorelativism: is the attitude that cultural difference is just different, without being better or worse

Evil Eye: a malevolent glare that acts like a curse and needs to be protected against through amulets and by avoiding to give others reason to be jealous

Intercultural Intelligence: describes the capability to act appropriately in diverse intercultural settings. Various proponents have tried to measure and describe it, see e.g. books by Earley and Ang (2003) as well as Livermore (2009)

Mana: is understood as the ability to achieve extraordinary things (Käser 2014b, 66ff)

Mary Douglas: was a British Anthropologist who developed a cultural theory based on social parameters. Weak vs. strong community (in this book Me- vs. Us-Cultures), and the degree of structure in society. She thus defined four cultural types, which in this book – following Silzer – are called: Institutionalizing (weak community, high structure through rules and schedule); Individuating (weak community, low structure); Hierarching (strong community, high structure through social distinctions); Interrelating (strong community, weak structure)

Multiple Intelligences: developed in the 1980s by Howard Gardner the theory of multiple intelligences is still a pedagogical concept today. Among others, linguistic, mathematic-logical or musical intelligences are counted among them (Gardner 2002, 69)

Patronage: (or patron-client relationship) is the interaction between two unequal partners, in which the patron provides material goods, and as the counterbalance, the client 'repays' the patron with mostly immaterial things such as honour, thanks and loyalty

Shame: the term used in the context of culture does not refer to psychological shame, but to a public disgrace, to being shunned, to the loss of reputation and face, to being excluded from the community. A person who has been shamed wants their **honour**, i.e. their standing within the group, to be restored

Worldview: is like a set of glasses through which we see and interpret the world

www.ingramcontent.com/pod-product-compliance
Lightning Source LLC
La Vergne TN
LVHW041339200726
843509LV00009B/777